CONGRESS

Keystone of the

Washington Establishment

MORRIS P. FIORINA

CONGRESS *Keystone of the Washington Establishment*

SECOND EDITION

Yale University Press
New Haven and London

Set in Times Roman type by The Composing Room of Michigan. Printed in the United States of America by Courier Companies, Inc.

Library of Congress Cataloging-in-Publication Data
Fiorina, Morris P.
Congress, keystone of the Washington establishment / Morris P. Fiorina.
— 2nd ed.
      p.   cm.
   Bibliography: p.
   Includes index.
   ISBN 0–300–04639–1. — ISBN 0–300–04640–5 (pbk.)
   1. United States. Congress.   2. Administrative agencies—United
States.   3. Representative government and representation—United
States.   I. Title.
JK1071.F55   1989
328.73—dc20   89–8919
                                                                   CIP

The paper in this book meets the guidelines for permanence and durability of the Committee on Production Guidelines for Book Longevity of the Council on Library Resources.

10   9   8   7   6   5

TO MY PARENTS —

HELEN & MO

Contents

Figures and Tables

FIGURES

TABLES

Preface to the Second Edition

The first edition of this book was written during the presidential campaigns of 1976 and published in 1977. From some perspectives, such as that of earth science, twelve years is the blink of an eye. But from the perspective of political analysis, twelve years can be an epoch. In these past twelve years the Reagan era has come and gone. The frustrating stagflation of the 1970s has given way to the variable prosperity of the 1980s, and the energy crisis dominates the news no more. Most important, thinking about Congress has changed in significant ways. As noted in the introduction to the first edition, the academic view of Congress was generally positive in 1976. The popular view, too, was more favorable than usual, reflecting the post-Watergate feeling that the system had indeed worked.

Judgments are not so positive as the 1980s draw to a close. The polls show that popular ratings of Congress have returned to their traditionally low levels,[1] and informed commentators have some unusually harsh things to say about Congress. Richard Reeves, for example, confesses that

> I begin 1988 more depressed than in any of my five previous national election years. I think American politics touched a new low last year. I don't mean the character and credentials of the six-packs of presidential candidates. . . . My depression (and anger) concerns the 100th Congress.

Reeves proceeds to detail a series of congressional transgressions.[2] Noting former Speaker Tip O'Neill's famous dictum that "all politics is local," Reeves continues:

> There is a calculating cynicism to O'Neill's remark, as if elected representatives have no higher responsibility than servicing their districts or their own re-election—or just the locality of their own interests or those of a few friends.

With a somewhat different focus but an equally critical eye, David Broder likens the Democratic-controlled House of Representatives to the Soviet bureaucratic state, and asks, "How about a little glasnost for the one-party House of Representatives?"[3]

Academic views, too, have shifted. Over the past decade numerous scholars have taken a more critical stance toward Congress. The general theme of their analyses is similar in spirit to that underlying the first edition: unconstrained pursuit of personal goals by members results in the failure of Congress to meet collective responsibilities.[4] Some scholars see a dynamic that makes things get better after they get sufficiently bad, but most are less sanguine.[5] The academic consensus has become sufficiently critical that a revisionist scholar now is one who writes a book arguing that Congress is not so bad as his colleagues think it is.[6] And cases in which Congress appears *not* to have succumbed to parochial pressures are now considered "man bites dog" stories worthy of publication. In this greatly altered intellectual environment I have at times been put in the position of strongly defending Congress—against policy analysts who would have expert bureaucrats run the country, and against lawyers who would have judges run it. What goes around comes around, and then some.

The altered political and intellectual environment has led me to return to this twelve-year-old book, to see what it actually said, how it has held up with the passage of time, and how new developments have intruded upon the original argument. The result is this second, enlarged edition. The first edition appears as part 1 of this edition. According to colleagues, over and above its substantive content *Keystone* (as it is commonly called) saw considerable use as a pedagogical device, a short (and cheap) example of how a political scientist defines a problem, evaluates hypotheses, formulates new ones, and draws implications. An expansion and reworking of the original essay would detract from that usage. Thus, I have constructed this second edition by preparing a second part made up of four new chapters. One discusses some pertinent evidence that was not available twelve years ago. A second addresses common misunderstandings of the original arguments. A third treats a number of topics whose importance has become apparent during the intervening twelve years, and a final chapter offers some current thoughts on Congress in particular and American politics in general as we move toward the twenty-first century.

As background to the four new chapters the reader might appreciate having some idea of the nature of the reaction to the first edition. The original introduction expressed concern that academic colleagues would not be receptive to an "avowedly critical" effort. But academic reaction to the book was on the whole positive—academics appreciate a provocative argument, whether they fully accept it or not. Charles O. Jones did decry the tendency toward "slam dunk" theories of Congress (leading one colleague to suggest changing my name to "Air" Fiorina), but the book became a staple of college courses on Congress in the 1980s.[7]

As for reaction in the larger world of public affairs, my original hope was that *Keystone* would be received as a nonpartisan, nonideological commentary. In retrospect this hope was monumentally naïve.[8] With a Congress seemingly under the permanent control of the Democrats, any criticism of that institution inevitably would be taken as partisan.[9] And so it was. The journal of the Republican National Committee, *Commensense,* published a review so positive as to make the rest of my literary life anticlimactic.[10] Perhaps as a consequence, Republican congressmen and staffers pushed the book. One southern Republican phoned to say that he was having the book distributed to all the political science departments in his district. (He went on to admit that he was the kind of congressman the book described, but that he had no choice if he wanted to keep his seat.) Several colleagues in the Midwest received copies from their congressmen. And prominent Republican politicos reportedly praised *Keystone* at various functions. A survey of press clippings indicates that numerous smaller (that is, Republican) newspapers lauded the book on their editorial pages. Democrats pointedly ignored it.

In the world of ideas, partisanship and ideology tend to go hand in hand. Not surprisingly, then, some critics perceived the hidden hand of right-wing ideology in the pages of *Keystone.* For Steven Kelman the book justifies my inclusion in a list of influential academic "rightists" including Gordon Tullock, William Niskanen, David Mayhew (!), and E. S. Savas.[11] Happily, undergraduates do not view the world so simplistically. When appearing before student audiences, I am frequently asked about my politics. For students find mixed signals in *Keystone:* some remarks and arguments suggest a rightward lean, while other observations belie such a bias. At the risk of injecting too personal a note into these pages, I will provide a brief outline of my political views. Given that the book's arguments have provoked speculation and suspicion about the values and opinions behind them, some background information seems appropriate.

I have never registered as a Republican nor voted for Ronald Reagan. More often than not, abstention or voting for a minor-party candidate has struck me as the best choice. As for the issues, over the years I have become more cautious about government intervention in economic affairs, not because of any blind belief that markets are perfect, but because of the evidence provided by reality. Advocates of government intervention too often offer wishful thinking and good intentions when realism and good analysis are what we need. Even more important, history provides too many examples of special-interest wolves wearing public-interest fleeces. Certainly there is a role for government in the economic realm, but the burden of proof should be heavier than the modern Democratic party has demanded. The principal exception I would make concerns the realm of environmental, health, and safety regulation, where obvious considerations make me more willing to err on the side of intervention.

If my skeptical stance on economic issues can be characterized as right-of-center, my thinking on defense spending and foreign policy leans in the other direction. If anything, I am more outraged by waste, fraud, and abuse in the defense sector than in the domestic sector. At least the beneficiaries in the latter area need it more than those in the former. As for broader policy questions, without going into detail, suffice it to say that isolationism has an undeserved bad name.

Finally, in the realm of the various social, moral, and cultural issues, my positions span the ideological spectrum in a fashion that would give little solace to either the New Right or the "Brookline-Cambridge crowd." The ERA? Yes. Capital punishment? Yes. Legalization of drugs? It should be considered.

American political life consists of a raucous, ongoing debate over where we are going as a society. No participant in that debate is free from bias, none has all the answers, none is right all the time. But this contribution to the debate is animated by the same spirit as the first edition of this book: my intent is nonpartisan and reformist. When understanding is increased, then in some small degree the prospects for improving our lot are increased as well.

Acknowledgments

A number of people contributed in a variety of ways to the writing of this book. My distinguished colleague John Ferejohn fanned the flames of my interest by impishly pointing out that recent trends in congressional elections were inconsistent with aspects of my earlier published work. My curiosity aroused, I prevailed upon the Division of the Humanities and Social Sciences at Caltech to fund the field trip described in chapter 4, although I could provide justification little more concrete that a hunch that I could learn something by going into the field. Another colleague, Charles Plott, encouraged me to communicate my developing ideas to a broad audience rather than bury them in the pages of specialized journals. These individuals and institutions got me going. My secretary, Georgeia Hutchinson, kept me going. Her rapid and steady pace prevented me from slacking off in the home stretch.

Numerous individuals read and commented on the manuscript. My wife, Mary, and good friends Rick and Merry Rossini flagged passages and tables that were incomprehensible to the nonspecialist. Graduate students Randy Calvert, Paul Thomas, and Barry Weingast egged me on, as did colleague Roger Noll. Other colleagues—John Aldrich, Herbert Asher, Robert Bates, Ken Shepsle, and Herbert Weisberg—reacted to my ideas, some more positively than others. (Bates, incidentally, rendered the valuable service of introducing me to the good people of Yale University Press.) Finally, day-to-day interaction with Burt Klein and Mel Hinich has affected my outlook in various ways. As usual, however, I absolve all of the above-named individuals of any direct responsibility for what ultimately appears on the pages that follow. Presumably they will privately claim credit for any ideas that gain general acceptance.

Most of all I thank my lovely wife, Mary, best friend and source of unswerving support.

CONGRESS

Keystone of the
Washington Establishment

PART ONE

Introduction to Part One

out-of-touch critics shall lead to "governing by the polls" [handwritten margin note]

The presidential campaigns of 1976 offered a curious spectacle: serious candidates for national office ran *for* Washington office by running *against* Washington.[1] They asked us to believe that the seat of national government is (choose): (a) immobile, (b) corrupt, (c) dangerously out of touch, (d) all of the above. The critics charged that the country is misgoverned by a Washington establishment, a Washington inner circle, or a group of Washington insiders. Such charges apparently carried a ring of truth; even Gerald Ford— twenty-eight years a member of the ruling circles—could not resist the temptation to attack Washington.

Wild charges fly in every election year of course. The theme that the government is wrongfully influenced by an unrepresentative, illegitimate, or even conspiratorial group surfaces quite regularly in American political campaigns. The Washington establishment can be viewed as a contemporary successor to the Slave Power, Wall Street, Merchants of Death, Malefactors of Great Wealth, the International Communist Conspiracy, and the Military Industrial Complex. Those seeking political power regularly create and use such symbols as elements of campaign strategy. But why should they do so unless such strategies periodically succeed? And why should conspiratorial symbols succeed unless candidates and others can marshal evidence consistent with some notion of inner circle rule?[2] And how can anyone offer generally convincing evidence unless at least a semblance of such inner circle rule exists? The concept of an international communist conspiracy never attained widespread credibility, rightfully so, and that notion now sits in the dustbin of political history. But candidates could and did persuade a large part of the electorate of the existence of a slave power, and a new party rode that issue to control of the national government. I humbly suggest that the Republicans' success of a century ago stemmed in no small part from the veracity of their charges.

This book makes a simple argument: the notion of a Washington establishment should not be dismissed as just another campaign slogan, a discomforting ghost conjured up by Ronald Reagan and Jimmy Carter in order to scare voters away from U.S. senators with presidential fever. I am convinced that something meriting the name of Washington establishment exists and that its continued operation has potentially disturbing implications for the future welfare of this country. I have written this short book in the hope of stimulating serious investigation and discussion of the workings of the Washington establishment. Otherwise the situation might escape the limelight once the heat of the campaign diminishes.

I have not written a topical work before, and it is with some uncertainty that I do so now: topical writing arouses suspicion in serious academic circles (although few serious academics decline the opportunity when it is urged upon them). I have written this book on a level midway between academic and lay audiences. On the one hand, the book is more systematic and more thoroughly documented than the typical ''pop'' book on politics. On the other hand, parts of the book are more theoretical (that is, speculative) than the typical academic study of Congress. Chapters 1–3 build on a firm foundation of academic research, but the remainder of the book relies more on examples and on the intuitive plausibility of the argument than on exhaustive data analyses.

The book differs from academic studies of Congress in one other major respect: its tone is openly critical. My fellow congressional scholars have written exhaustively about the positive aspects of our national legislature. Much of what they have written I agree with. But I believe that they have been less thorough in analyzing the negative side of Congress. I trust that one avowedly critical effort will not destroy the balance.

The plan of the book is somewhat circuitous. I will ask the reader to follow me along an intellectual and physical path that begins with a question bearing no apparent relation to the existence of a Washington establishment. I followed this path to that conclusion, and I hope to convince the reader to do likewise. Before proceeding, let me equip the reader with a summary description of what lies at the end of our path.

There is a Washington establishment. In fact, it is a hydra with each head only marginally concerned with the others' existence. These establishments are *not* malevolent, centrally directed conspiracies against the American people. Rather, they are unconsciously evolved and evolving networks of congressmen, bureaucrats, and organized subgroups of the citizenry all seeking to achieve their own goals. Contrary to what is popularly believed, the bureaucrats are not the problem. Congressmen are. *The Congress is the key to the Washington establishment.* The Congress created the establishment, sustains it, and most likely will continue to sustain and even expand it. But I emphasize again that the disturbing aspects of the Washington establishment follow from the uncoordinated operations of the overall system, not from any sinister motivation of those who compose it. The perceptive observer can identify the actors, specify their motives, and analyze their methods of operation. But many of those in the heart of the establishment are genuinely unaware that they are members in good standing.

DOONESBURY

by Garry Trudeau

Chapter 1

The Case of the Vanishing Marginals (with apologies to David Mayhew)

Throughout the postwar period we have heard jokes about the length of congressional careers. Most of these come in connection with discussions of the congressional seniority system, which purportedly elevates ancient southern congressmen to chairmanships of the standing committees of Congress.[1] Behind the jokes there stand hard facts. Congress today is occupied by career politicians. Generally speaking the only congressmen who do not intend to spend the rest of their careers in Congress are those senators who hope to move up to the presidency. Since World War II nearly 90 percent of all incumbents have sought reelection in any given election, and approximately 90 percent of all those who ran were successful.[2] There have been exceptions of course. The elections of 1958, 1964, and 1974 were a bit rougher on incumbents than usual. And voluntary retirement rates jumped in the early 1970s under the stimulus of significant improvements in congressional pensions and the unpleasantries of holding office during the Watergate period. But despite this recent infusion of fresh blood, we have every reason to believe that the new congressmen intend to match the careers of the older ones they replaced.

The professionalization of Congress is a twentieth-century phenomenon.[3] During the nineteenth century congressional turnover consistently amounted to 40–50 percent of the membership at each election, sometimes going even higher (73 percent in 1843, 61 percent in 1853, 58 percent in 1875). Not until the turn of the century did the average continuous service of congressmen climb to five years. The seniority system itself postdates the 1909–11 revolt in the House, although it arose somewhat earlier in the Senate. In an era in which congressmen had no seniority, the system made no sense.

What factors transformed the unstable Congress of the nineteenth century into the professionalized Congress of the twentieth? A variety of influences have been identified. The realignment of the 1890s effectively ended two-

Chapters 1–9 were written during the presidential campaigns of 1976.

party competition in many areas of the country, particularly the South, but in parts of the North and Midwest as well. Fewer congressmen went down to defeat under these conditions. But there was also a large voluntary component to the change. During the early nineteenth century, Washington was a provincial rural village set off in a swampy river bottom. Congressmen regularly abandoned their posts for the more pleasant conditions of public office in the relatively more cosmopolitan state capitals.[4] Sometimes congressmen had to leave office to repair their personal finances—Congress was a penurious body in those days (with good reason: congressional turnover rose 15 percent following a pay raise in 1816). In the home districts the congressional nomination was sometimes viewed as an honor to be spread among the good citizens of the district. Abraham Lincoln, for example, was denied renomination to Congress; he had already had his turn.

As the nineteenth century passed, conditions changed. The power and significance of the national government increased steadily, particularly following the Civil War. By 1890 it was no longer true that the Virginia State Legislature was more important than the U.S. Congress. The typical congressman had relatively fewer attractive career opportunities outside Washington. Facing these changed conditions, he responded by more frequent attempts to attain reelection and, not at all incidentally, to gain a greater degree of control over his destiny. The 1910 revolt, from which followed the contemporary seniority system, can be interpreted as an attempt by the rank and file to reduce the uncertainty surrounding a congressional career.[5] By breaking the arbitrary power of the party leadership and substituting an automatic leadership selection system, individual congressmen could plan a congressional career in a manner not previously possible. Seniority, in turn, interacted with congressional turnover. A congressman could no longer take periodic leaves of office to repair his finances or just to vacation. To do so would be to forfeit his seniority. District political elites could no longer afford to rotate the congressional nomination. Such practices would penalize their districts within the congressional power structure. The longer a congressman stayed in Washington, the greater his incentive to stay longer. The seniority system is misunderstood. Its principal effect is not that it selects old and unrepresentative congressmen to chair the committees; the system encourages old and unrepresentative congressmen generally and deprives local districts of any incentive to replace them with younger, more qualified, and more representative individuals.

The preceding discussion provides some general background on the Congress and how it has developed over time. Let us now examine some developments that have occurred more recently and over a time span measured in decades, not centuries.

Between 1940 and 1970 congressional turnover continued to decline, although the change was slight compared to what had already occurred. During this period turnover declined from about one-fourth of the members of the House to about one-sixth, even slipping below 10 percent in the election of 1968. (In 1974 turnover was comparatively high, 21 percent, but this figure was lower than that recorded in nine of ten elections between 1930 and 1950. And in 1976, turnover dropped back to about 15 percent.) What accounts for this contemporary decline? Changes in the congressional context offer no clues, and the increasing congressional membership stability occurs at a time when the electorate is growing increasingly volatile at the presidential level.

The key to this small puzzle was provided by Professor David Mayhew in an article subtitled "The Case of the Vanishing Marginals."[6] Political scientists traditionally use the term *marginal district* to refer to those congressional districts not firmly in the camp of one party or the other. *Swing district* is another commonly used term. *Safe districts,* of course, are those which are not marginal. Customarily, marginal districts are identified by victory percentages of 50–55 percent. In this range a particularly strong effort by a challenger, a weak effort by the incumbent, or a national swing against the incumbent's party may be enough to swing the district from one party's camp into the other's. In the recent past marginal districts have accounted for the bulk of the change in the membership in Congress—national swings such as those occurring in 1946 and 1964 exact a high toll in congressmen from such districts.

Mayhew's important observation was a simple one: the marginal district is going the way of the passenger pigeon.

In figure 1 I have excerpted some of Mayhew's data. The left-hand graphs record the percentage of the vote attained by Democratic congressional candidates in each of the congressional districts contested by an incumbent. To read the 1948 graph, for example, in 15 percent of the districts the Democratic candidate got 45–50 percent of the vote, in 12 percent of the districts he received 50–55 percent of the vote, in 15 percent of the districts he received 95–100 percent of the vote (mostly uncontested southern districts), and so forth. The proportion of marginal districts, of course, is given by the height of the bars in the middle of the graph in the area of 50 percent Democratic. In the

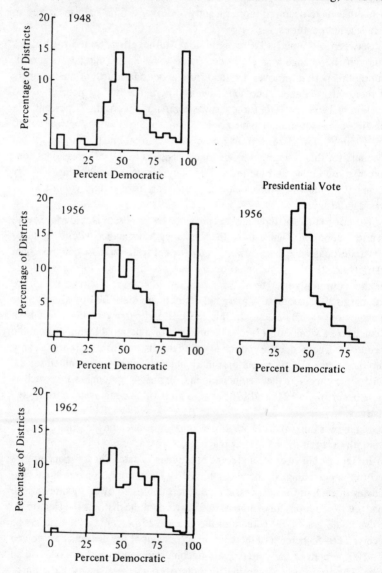

Figure 1. Congressional Vote in Districts with Incumbents Running, 1948–72

Figure 1—*Continued*

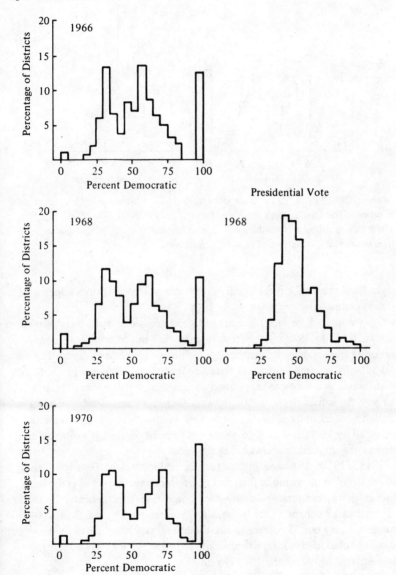

Figure 1–*Continued*

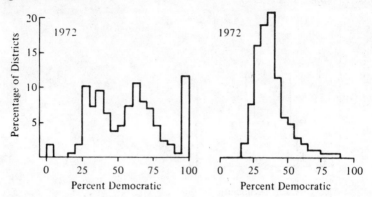

Source: The 1956 to 1972 data are drawn from David Mayhew, ''Congressional Elections: The Case of the Vanishing Marginals,'' *Polity* 6 (1974): 295–317. The 1948 data are drawn from the 1948 *Congressional Quarterly Almanac* and the Congressional Quarterly *Guide to U.S. Elections.*

right-hand graphs the presidential vote by congressional district appears for (later) comparative purposes.

When we look through the series of figures constructed by Mayhew, what do we find? In 1948 most of the districts fall in the competitive range. Ignoring the uncontested districts, as we depart further and further from a 50-50 split we find fewer and fewer congressional districts. In 1956 the distribution is a bit more ragged and asymmetric, but the overall picture is largely the same. In the 1960s, however, changes are clearly evident. A trough appears in the area of a 50-50 split in 1962 and becomes quite pronounced by 1966. It is as if someone had stepped on the 1948 distribution, depressing the middle and swelling the ends.

By the 1970s the bimodality had become strikingly clear. Fewer and fewer districts fall in the swing or marginal range. More and more fall in the range that is quite comfortable—safe—for congressional incumbents. In 1972 fewer than 25 percent of the incumbents who ran won by less than a 60-40 margin. Using our 55 percent rule of thumb, 90 percent of all 1972 winners would be classified as safe, whereas only 75 percent would have been similarly classified following the 1948 election.[7]

Seldom in the social sciences do data speak so clearly. Mayhew's figures provide us with a partial answer: congressional turnover has declined in the postwar period because the kind of district that produces the lion's share of that turnover is disappearing. This partial answer, however, raises two additional questions. First, why are the marginal districts disappearing? Second, why should anyone care? Answering the first question starts us down the path that leads to the Washington establishment. Answering the second provides the motivation to follow that path. So, let us briefly consider the significance of marginal districts before returning to the main lines of the analysis.

① NELs — what is the electoral
incentive? Get the
drug-use or gay-vote?

Chapter 2

The Marginal District: Some Brief Remarks about the Victim

Upon casual consideration of the lot of a marginal district congressman, we are likely to feel a touch of sympathy. Here is a would-be statesman elected by 52 or 53 percent of the vote who lives in mortal fear for his political life. One mistake on a roll-call vote, one slip of the tongue, one touch of scandal, an unpopular presidential candidate put forward by his party or a popular one by the opposition—any such factor might return him to the law office in the county seat. He lives insecurely with the knowledge that ambitious members of both district parties savor his electoral weakness and impatiently await any small signal that this is *the time* to take him on.

Our initial sympathetic reaction is probably a mistake, however. The marginal congressman is analogous to the rabbit in a natural ecosystem: his life is hard in a world full of coyotes, but he's necessary for the health of the overall system.

The marginal congressman provides the means by which changes in popular sentiments receive expression in the halls of the Capitol.[1] Safe district congressmen come and stay (until voluntary retirement or moral indiscretion opens up their seat). An electoral debacle on the part of their party's presidential candidate might depress their percentage of the vote from 65 to 60 percent. An all-out challenge within the district might do likewise. But generally speaking the safe congressman observes the ebb and flow of political debate in the country as something of an uninvolved observer. Popular wisdom portrays the congressman as weak and vacillating, one who sways with every political breeze. But academic studies suggest to the contrary that incumbent congressmen maintain a marked stability in their positions over time.[2] If you wish to know how a congressman is voting in 1970, the chances are very good that his 1960 voting record will tell you. *As a consequence, the only reliable way to achieve policy change in Congress is to change congressmen.* And here the marginal district enters.

The existence of marginal districts builds necessary responsiveness into the electoral system. Whether coming to Washington on the coattails of a

14

popular president (1964) or over the bodies of the congressional victims of an unpopular one (1974), the marginal district congressmen constitute the electoral mandate. Consider, for example, some data on the comparative voting records of the 1964 marginal congressmen and those whom they defeated (37 districts were involved).[3]

Average Decrease in Conservative Coalition Support   61%
Average Increase in Support for a Larger Federal Role   51%

The Conservative Coalition Support Score is a general measure of conservatism based on all those votes in which Republicans and southern Democrats coalesce against northern Democrats. The Larger Federal Role Support Score is a generalized Liberalism Score. (Both of these scores are compiled by *Congressional Quarterly,* an independent research organization.) Clearly the new congressmen, almost all of whom were Democrats, voted in dramatically different fashion from the congressmen they defeated. On the average they were 61 percent less supportive of the conservative coalition and 51 percent more supportive of federal intervention in society than those whom they replaced. One may credit the political leadership of Lyndon Johnson for the legislation passed by the 89th Congress, but one should not forget the replacement of a significant number of conservative Republicans by liberal Democrats. The importance of those votes is apparent when we consider the differences between the voting records of marginal Republicans and those whom they defeated in 1966 (29 districts were involved):

Average Increase in Conservative Coalition Support   58%
Average Decrease in Support for a Larger Federal Role   43%

Undoubtedly, Johnson was a less effective leader in the 90th Congress. But he also had thirty fewer liberals and thirty more conservatives to try to lead.

The significance of the marginal district is clear in any discussion of electoral mandates. Even on a smaller scale, though, the importance of the marginals should not be ignored. Those in a district who are dissatisfied with their congressman must beat him, not persuade him. And they have a chance only in a marginal district. *As such districts disappear we face the possibility of a Congress composed of professional officeholders oblivious to the changing political sentiments of the country.*

Of course we must be careful not to treat the distinction between marginal and safe districts as something ordained by God. Why are some districts marginal and others not? The traditional explanation is based on the relative socioeconomic homogeneity or heterogeneity of the district.[4] A black central city district is not likely to have a healthy Republican organization. Nor is a WASP, small-townish New England or midwestern district likely to have a flourishing Democratic party. Marginal districts have tended to be those whose socioeconomic structure provides a base for both parties—an agricultural area containing a medium-sized industrial city, a district originally settled by New England pietists and later invaded by Lutherans and Catholics, a metropolitan district containing both wealthy suburbs and ethnic blue-collar neighborhoods. Some politically relevant social or economic cleavage that divides the district into relatively equal parts has been viewed as a necessary condition for a district to fall into the marginal class.

Within the boundaries set by socioeconomic conditions, individual congressmen may of course take actions that advance or impair their electoral fortunes. A basically marginal district might appear safe when held by some particularly effective incumbent, just as a basically safe district might appear marginal when held by some particularly ineffective one. Congressmen are not passive, powerless robots randomly selected from the district's population. Thus the disappearance of the marginals suggests that we examine two factors: (1) possible changes in the socioeconomic homogeneity of congressional districts, (2) possible changes in the effectiveness of congressional incumbents. In the next chapter we will consider the first possibility and reject it. In later chapters we will see how incumbents have managed to structure Washington influence relationships so as to make their reelections ever more certain.

Chapter 3
The Vanishing Marginals: Who Done It?

Is there any basis for arguing that the disappearance of the marginals stems from the increasing socioeconomic homogeneity of congressional districts? On the face of it the charge is dubious. Socioeconomic change tends to be gradual; it takes decades to show up. The decline of the marginals, however, has been fairly rapid. In the late 1950s everything looked normal. By 1970 something had happened.

Could it be that socioeconomic cleavage lines have become less politically relevant? Again, the suggestion is doubtful. Dormant religious differences were awakened in 1960. The New Deal class cleavages were sharpened and reinforced in the 1964 election. Race came to the fore during all the mid-sixties elections. If anything, socioeconomic cleavages became more politically relevant during the 1960s.[1]

A more sophisticated argument relies on the observation that congressional districts do not just "happen" to be more or less homogeneous in a socioeconomic sense. Rather, a district's characteristics in some part depend on the actions of the state legislature, which draws the district's boundaries. Within limits, the state legislature can choose how homogeneous and therefore how competitive its congressional districts will be. Consider a hypothetical state of one thousand voters, half of whom are blue-collar workers who typically vote for the alpha party, half of whom are white-collar workers who typically vote for the omega party. If the voters are mixed evenly throughout the state's population, any drawing of district boundaries would produce closely divided (marginal) districts. But suppose that the blue-collar workers live together in the northern half of the state, while the white-collar workers live together in the southern half of the state. In this case the state legislature has a great deal of influence on the shape of the state's congressional elections. Assume the state is to be divided into ten districts of equal population which meet the modern requirements of contiguity and compactness. Then the legislature could draw congressional districts lines vertically (north to south) and produce ten marginal districts each containing 50 percent alpha voters (in the northern half) and 50 percent omega voters (in the south-

District

1	2	3	4	5	6	7	8	9	10
			B	L	U	E			
		W	H	I	T	E			

ern half). (See the first diagram.) But on the other hand, the legislature could just as easily draw the district boundaries horizontally, thereby producing ten safe districts, five containing only alpha voters, five containing only omega voters. (See the second diagram.) Clearly, if this hypothetical state were to change its districting arrangement from the first case to the second, ten marginals would disappear.

To be sure, the conditions of our hypothetical example are not fully met in the real world. Groups are not monolithic in their political allegiances, nor do they congregate in ethnically or otherwise pure regions. But groups do have political leanings, and their members do tend to live together rather than to

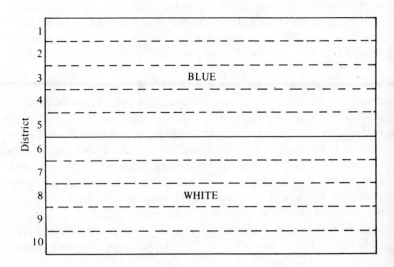

mix randomly in the population. Thus legislatures can exert great influence on the shape of the state's congressional elections, although not absolute influence as in the hypothetical example.

Considerations like the preceding suggest the hypothesis that changed redistricting strategies have reduced the number of marginal districts. The U.S. Supreme Court's "one man, one vote" decisions directly stimulated widespread redistricting during the mid to late 1960s.[2] Some political scientists trace the decline of the marginals directly to the court-ordered redistrictings. Professor Edward Tufte, for example, refers to the latter as "incumbent protection acts."[3]

Is redistricting the guilty factor? The time periods link up very nicely—the bulk of the decline in marginal districts occurs just as redistricting is at a fever pitch. Moreover, state legislatures clearly recognize the political possibilities inherent in redistricting, as innumerable legislative stalemates and gubernatorial vetoes testify. But still, is there a reasonable doubt?

One question we might ask is, "Why the 1960s?" The states typically redistrict (or at least have the justification to redistrict) following each dicennial census. Why then would they not get rid of the marginals in the 1940s or 1950s? Why wait until the 1960s, especially given that politically tricky redistricting was probably *easier* prior to the Supreme Court decisions, which do after all rule out the most blatant attempts to gain political advantage by tinkering with district boundaries? Why the 1960s? Are we to believe that state legislators loved and protected their congressmen more in 1965 than in 1955?

Another problem arises when we consider the distributions of the *presidential* vote in the nation's congressional districts (chapter 1). If state legislatures had simply redistricted the country into more homogeneous, safe districts, then we should pick up the same kind of bimodal pattern in the presidential vote that we do in the congressional. But we don't. The distribution of the presidential vote continues to be unimodal in 1968 and 1972, although it lists well to the shy side of 50 percent Democratic under the impact of the McGovern disaster. Can districts be designed so that they are safe for one party in congressional elections but not in presidential elections? I am dubious. In my mind a reasonable doubt about the responsibility of bipartisan redistricting has been established. And the defense has not yet rested its case.

Professor John Ferejohn presents data that cut to the heart of the matter.[4] Tufte had shown that certain large states which redistricted during the mid-sixties have fewer marginal districts after the redistricting than they had prior *maybe redistricting was only used ... were marginal districts were not naturally disappearing, as in Ferejohn's "cont..."*

20   *THE VANISHING MARGINALS: WHO DONE IT?*

to the redistricting. Ferejohn asks the natural question, "What happened in those states which did not redistrict during the same time period?" He constructs table 1. Evidently redistricting is innocent. The marginals were disappearing just as rapidly when redistricting was not taking place as when it was. In separate studies Professors Charles Bullock and Albert Cover provide additional evidence that exonerates redistricting.[5] The defense rests.

In chapter 2 I suggested that two kinds of changes were candidates for an explanation of the vanishing marginals. The first, change in the socioeconomic heterogeneity of congressional districts, we have just considered and rejected. The second involves not congressional districts, but congressmen themselves. Are incumbents more effective now than previously? If so, why?

Professor Robert Erikson has conducted research that provides statistical estimates of the "incumbency effect," the extra percentage of the vote that appears to result simply from being an incumbent, and not from party membership, region, election year, and other factors.[6] Erikson concludes that during the 1950s and early 1960s the incumbency effect was statistically present but politically unimportant. He estimates the effect as between 1 and 2 percent of the congressional vote. But, as we have seen before, something happened during the mid-1960s. Erikson's estimates for this period jump to 5 percent. The typical marginal district congressman is no longer marginal when he runs for reelection after a term in office. How can we account for this significant increase in the value of incumbency?

One possibility involves the growing pool of resources available to incumbent congressmen but not to their opponents. Congressmen have always had the visibility that accompanies victory in one or more congressional races.

Table 1. Decline in Percentage of Marginal Districts in Non-Southern States

1962–66	State Redistricted	State Not Redistricted
1962	51%	51%
1966	40	28
1966–70		
1966	35%	39%
1970	27	33

After all, just being a winner is testimony to having achieved some minimum threshold of visibility in the district. Moreover, once in office the congressman can advertise. The newspapers and local radio and TV cover his positions on important legislation. Awards of projects and grants within his district are channeled through his office. He may write a short column or tape a short Washington report for the local media. He can use the congressional frank to shower his constituents with questionnaires and newsletters, letters of congratulation and condolence, pamphlets on child care and vegetable gardens, free seeds, and various other missives. Congressmen certainly use these opportunities to communicate with their districts. Moreover, they are using these opportunities at an increasing rate. Consider figure 2, which details the volume of franked mail during the period of interest.

Figure 2. Franked Mail Sent out by House and Senate Members, 1954–70

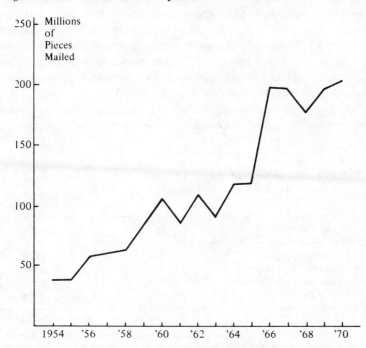

Source: Mayhew, "The Case of the Vanishing Marginals."

Evidently the use of the frank has increased remarkably in recent years, far exceeding the increase in the population of congressional districts. Notice too that the trend line rockets skyward between 1963 and 1966, precisely the time when the marginals were disappearing. (For the curious I might inject parenthetically that when the data are broken down by month, one sees that October of even-numbered years is a hot time in the old Capitol Hill Post Office.) Could the explanation for the vanishing marginals be a very simple matter of advertising? Congressmen advertise more now than they did twenty years ago and get more votes now than they did twenty years ago.

This explanation is not very complimentary to the American electorate: it suggests that citizens vote on the basis of simple name recognition. But the explanation cannot be rejected out of hand. Voting studies have typically found that "to be known at all is to be known favorably."[7] An important study carried out in 1958, for example, produced table 2.

The implications of table 2 are really rather striking. Those voters who had *no information whatsoever* on the congressional race in their district typically cast a party-line vote; about 90 percent of them did so. If the only information a voter had was about his own party's candidate, he was virtually certain to vote for that candidate. But information about the opposition party's candidate went along with a noticeable swing in support for him. In fact, those citizens who had information only about the opposition party candidate were practically an even bet to vote for him.

If we combine the preceding findings with the data on increased advertising by congressmen, we can construct the following argument. Incumbent

Table 2. Percentage of Party Identifiers Voting for Own Party Candidate in 1958, Contested Districts Only

Voter Aware of:	*%*	*No. of Voters*
Own candiate only	98	(166)
Neither candidate	92	(368)
Both candidates	83	(196)
Other candidates only	60	(68)

Source: Donald Stokes and Warren Miller, "Party Government and the Saliency of Congress," *Public Opinion Quarterly* 26 (1962): 631–46.

congressmen increasingly are finding ways to contact the citizens in their districts. Such contacts produce near perfect support among members of their own party and a much higher than expected level of support from among members of the opposition party. (Referring to the table, the argument is that incumbents are moving people out of the second category into the first and fourth categories.) As I have suggested, the argument is not very complimentary to the electorate. Can a vote really be bought by a letter of congratulation upon a high school graduation? By a district poll?

The argument has a more serious problem than whether we like it, however; other data exist that cast grave doubts upon its validity. If the argument were correct, we would expect to see the name recognition of congressional incumbents increasing over the period during which the marginals were vanishing. Do we? Consider table 3. The table reports data from academic surveys conducted under the auspices of the University of Michigan Center for Political Studies. What it shows is that incumbents are no better known following the era of the disappearing marginals than they were before it. And the differential advantage of the incumbent over the challenger, if anything, has lessened between the 1950s and the 1970s. Incumbents do have an advantage over challengers in terms of name recognition, but that advantage has eroded at the same time that the incumbency advantage in congressional elections has increased.

In sum, Common Cause, the League of Women Voters, and other ''public'' interest groups may deplore the existence of congressional ''perks''

Table 3. Voter Awareness of House Candidates in Contested Districts, 1958-74

	Aware of Incumbent	Aware of Challenger	Comparative Advantage of Incumbent
1958	58%	38%	+20%
1964	63	40	+23
1966	56	38	+18
1968	64	47	+17
1970	55	31	+24
1974	60	44	+16

Source: Ferejohn, "On the Decline of Competition."

such as the frank which seemingly give incumbents an unfair advantage. But there is no indication in the data that incumbents really profit greatly from the use of their perks, although they certainly do make use of them. We really have no choice but to release a second suspect for lack of evidence.

We are not yet out of suspects, however. Those researchers who have gathered the data that cast doubt on the explanations so far considered have put forth their own explanation for the decline of the marginals. This third explanation denies that state legislatures or public-relations-minded congressmen are behind the vanishing marginals. Rather, the voters are responsible: voters have changed the principles on which their congressional votes depend. In order to discuss this third argument I must digress briefly to present some general background on American voting behavior.

The classic voting studies carried out during the 1950s stressed the importance of party identification for a comprehensive explanation of American voting behavior.[8] The studies held that party identification is a psychological attachment to one of the two major parties. In the 1950s these identifications appeared to be very stable—people did not change their identification even when they decided to vote for the candidate of the other party. Moreover, party identification was the single best predictor of the vote, although by no means perfect. (Some Democrats did vote for Eisenhower, and 20 percent of the population did not identify with either party.) These findings about presidential voting appeared to have stark analogues on the congressional level. The evidence seemed conclusive that the congressional vote, particularly during mid-term elections, was a party-line vote.[9] In the general absence of information about the congressional candidates, most citizens simply voted for the candidate bearing the label of the party with which they identified. Turn back to table 1 in this chapter. Taking the table as a whole, 88 percent of the 789 voters included in the table voted consistently with their party identification. The decision rule for a congressional vote seemed to be a simple one: which candidate is the Democrat/Republican? Vote for him.

Alas, the world turns, and yesterday's truth is today's fiction. As the 1960s progressed political scientists increasingly came to see that the findings of the 1950s voting studies did not extend to all times and places.[10] The 1960s voter seemed different in several important ways from the 1950s voter. He was not so likely to have a party identification: the number of self-identified independents approximately doubled between the mid-fifties and today. Even those with a party identification were not so likely to follow it when making their voting decisions. The 1960s voter seemed to have more information about the issues and candidates and to use such information when he voted. And why not? The 1960s witnessed the rise of issues that impinged on the everyday lives of American citizens. These issues, moreover, cut across existing party alignments. A Democratic president sent the sons of the working class to die in a far away war. The urban strongholds of the Democratic party degenerated into a battleground where race fought race and criminals plundered society. Meanwhile, the adolescent children of the upper middle class gleefully seized the opportunity to overthrow moral and behavioral standards which their parents evaded but generally accepted. Facing such conditions a party identification based on the Great Depression seemed increasingly removed from the politics of the 1960s. Some disillusioned party identifiers moved into the ranks of the independents. And large numbers of the maturing baby boom, finding little that was relevant to their concerns in the existing party system, did likewise.

Posed against the stability of the 1950s was the instability of the late 1960s. A moribund Republican party came out of the grave dug in 1964 and floored the country's "majority" party in 1968. A strong third party movement arose and threatened to materially affect the outcome of the 1968 election. We heard talk of "emerging Republican majorities," the end of two-party politics, the decomposition of parties, and other grand changes.[11] Indisputably, times had changed.

In this context several researchers propounded a third explanation for the decline of the marginals, an explanation based on the behavioral changes that were occurring in the American electorate. Professors Walter Burnham, Robert Erikson, John Ferejohn, and others suggested that the intense and unstable national politics of the 1960s pushed some part of the citizenry into abandoning old principles of congressional voting, party identification in particular.[12] Advocates of this behavioral change view suggested that party identification traditionally had served as a "cue," or rule of thumb, to guide voting when the voter had little other information. So long as the parties stand for somewhat contrasting policies on issues of some concern to the voter, adherence to such cues is not a bad way to make voting decisions, particularly in obscure contests, as congressional races must seem to most people. But by the late 1960s many individuals could well have second thoughts about the rationality of employing party identification as a rule of thumb. One could very well unknowingly cast a vote for a radiclib or a neanderthal, as the case might be. With everything topsy-turvy on the presidential level, could one rely on party identification any longer?

Those who advocate the behavioral change view answer the preceding question in the negative or at least argue that some significant portion of the electorate answers the question in the negative. Assume for the moment, then, that some voters abandoned their usual rule of thumb—party identification—and voted on some other basis. What other basis is there? Incumbency, perhaps? The voter might reason that if he has heard nothing about the incumbent then the latter is probably not a wild man or woman, just some ordinary, reasonably satisfactory congressman. If that is the case, why change? Let the present incumbent stay in office until he makes some misstep sufficiently serious to justify chancing the unknown evils of the challenger. In sum, advocates of the behavioral change view contend that a significant part of the electorate has substituted incumbency for party identification as a simple principle on which to base a congressional vote.

Do we accept the behavioral change view, or can we raise a reasonable doubt? Certainly the view is consistent with the broad outlines of what has happened in congressional elections. Fewer and fewer congressional votes are party-line votes, as demonstrated in table 4. From the data in table 4 we see that there has been an 8-10 percent drop in the percentage of party-line votes between the mid-fifties and 1970. Our earlier table 2 represented something of a high point for party-line voting (1958). The shifts detailed in table 4 are not monumental, of course, but the decline of the marginals does not necessarily imply large shifts. If a congressman wins by 52 percent of the vote, then picks up an additional 5 percent in the next election, he is no longer marginal. Clearly the data in table 4 allow room for that degree of change to take place.

Table 4. Percentage of Party-Line Votes in House Elections

1956	82	1966	76
1958	84	1968	74
1960	80	1970	76
1962	83	1972	74
1964	79	1974	74

Source: Robert B. Arsenau and Raymond Wolfinger, "Voting Behavior in Congressional Elections," paper delivered at the annual meeting of the American Political Science Association, New Orleans, 1973. Supplemented with University of Michigan CPS Election Studies.

*not exactly – maybe
just 'smart' enough to
reject party-line voting.*

Still, there are questions that must be faced. The behavioral change view has an internally paradoxical quality about it. Supposedly party identification is declining in importance because voters have more information about the issues and candidates on which to base their votes. The electorate is a bit more alert and informed than it used to be. Isn't it somewhat curious that this same electorate would turn to the rather simpleminded rule of voting for incumbents? In essence, advocates of the behavioral change view would have us believe that congressional voting behavior has gotten dumber because the electorate has gotten smarter. A curious argument, I would say.

Even more serious, I think, is the existence of an abundance of data documenting the increasing alienation and cynicism of the American people. Professor Arthur Miller has analyzed much of this data.[13] He reports that between 1964 and 1970 trust in the government in Washington dropped 25 percent, beliefs that the government caters to a few big interests rose 20 percent, beliefs that the government habitually wastes money rose more than 20 percent, confidence in the competence of government officials dropped 17 percent. Even more to the point, a Harris survey found that between 1966 and 1973 confidence in the U.S. House of Representatives dropped 13 percent and in the Senate 12 percent.[14] Such data clearly show that the American citizenry is increasingly dubious about government intentions, competence, and efficiency. But advocates of the behavioral change view are arguing that these same citizens are increasingly supportive of the objects of their cynicism. The juxtaposition of these arguments casts a cloud of implausibility over the simple behavioral change view. Again, a reasonable doubt has been established.

*scope
shift –
Congress
✓
their
Congressmen*

All of the evidence discussed in this chapter has referred to elections for the U.S. House of Representatives. What of the Senate? Is the decline of the marginals purely a House phenomenon, or is a similar phenomenon apparent in Senate elections? Political scientists have examined the House much more closely than the Senate. There are 435 House elections every two years, enough to insure that idiosyncratic variation will cancel out and allow general patterns to emerge. In contrast, there are only thirty to thirty-five Senate elections every two years, and the greater visibility and media attention to the candidates and races create more variability in the results. Nevertheless, Professor Warren Kostroski has published a study which suggests that the Senate has undergone the same kind of change that is more clearly evident in the House.[15] Recall that Erikson estimated that the House incumbency effect jumped from less than 2 percent to 5 percent in the mid-sixties. Kostroski produces estimates of the independent effect of incumbency in Senate elections that show even more dramatic change. For Democratic senators Kostroski estimates an incumbency effect of 4 percent in 1948–52, increasing steadily to 12 percent in 1966–70. For Republicans the increase is from 1 percent to 11 percent over the same period. Needless to point out, senators' constituencies—states—are not subject to redistricting—one final nail in the coffin of the redistricting argument.

What do we have to show for this lengthy hunt for the people, events, or conditions that are responsible for the disappearing marginals? Nothing that is sufficient to convict, so to speak. We know that some kind of incumbency effect exists and apparently has come to exert an increasingly important influence on Congressional elections. But we cannot specify the exact nature of this effect, nor can we explain why it has grown stronger over time.

We have picked up some clues, however. We know that voters are not following their party identifications in their congressional voting as much as they used to. We know that congressmen are advertising more. We know that name recognition of the incumbent has not increased. We know that the most apparent institutional change—redistricting—can be ruled out. But what explanation is consistent with these clues? Why have the marginals disappeared? Perhaps we can find additional clues by interrogating two districts, one marginal, one ex-marginal. A study of two districts obviously cannot provide sufficient evidence for a conviction, but it might be enough to get another indictment.

Chapter 4
A Tale of Two Districts

Each of us has had the experiences of searching very hard for something only to find it right under our noses. After reading and pondering the studies on which the preceding chapter is based, I began to wonder whether some analogous oversight was occurring in the search for the cause(s) of the vanishing marginals. Could there be some obvious factor that our search was overlooking, some major change that would be apparent to anyone who took a detailed look at a few selected congressional districts rather than a gross look at all districts? Believing the effort to be worth the try, I decided to do a case study of two carefully chosen congressional districts. This study involved the usual examination of the electoral returns and demographic characteristics of the districts. But in addition to these standard methods, I decided to visit the districts, to walk the same streets and travel the same roads as the congressional candidates, and to talk to some of the same people whom they talk to.

Obvious criteria guided the selection of the districts. I wanted a vanishing marginal for one of the two. How do the local observers explain the changes that have occurred between the late fifties and the present? For the second district I chose one of the few remaining marginals, a district which has easily been one of the five most competitive congressional districts in the country during the postwar period. What might distinguish this rare survivor from the district that joined the ranks of the safe ones during the 1960s?

Other considerations could not be ignored. The districts should come from the same region; it would be foolish to choose one district from the South and one from the Northeast, say, because of other differing political trends in those regions. If possible, the districts should come from within the same state. Thus voters within the districts would have been faced with the same menu of choices in both presidential and state-level elections. It would be nice if the districts had reasonably similar demographic profiles; if one had more cows than people, and the other never saw a cow uncooked, inference might be rendered difficult. Requirements like these narrowed the set of interesting districts fairly quickly.

Fortunately, I was able to locate two districts that met the criteria outlined above. After general background research on the districts, I visited each for a week to observe the local scene first hand and discuss the district's congressional politics with local party officials, newspaper reporters, excongressmen, defeated congressional candidates, state legislators from districts within the congressional districts, and district staff employees of the incumbent congressmen. Their views were not always mutually consistent, far from it, but they were the source of a wealth of detailed information and tantalizing hypotheses. In order to protect the anonymity of those to whom I spoke (and to allow my colleagues the fun of guessing) I will refer to the two districts simply as district A and district B.

As indicated, both districts are in the same state. Neither would be classified as metropolitan nor rural. Rather, each contains a medium-sized city and an important agricultural sector. Both districts include more than two entire counties within their boundaries. From a demographic standpoint, there is little to choose between the two districts. Their occupational, educational, and income profiles are quite similar. Neither district contains a large minority population, although there were some racial incidents in district A during the late sixties. District B has a heavier concentration of southern and eastern European immigrant stock than does district A. The religious breakdowns of the two districts are similar, however. In short, a gross look at the characteristics of the two districts does not reveal any striking differences that might correspond to the dramatic disparity in their congressional election results since the mid-sixties.

Electorally, the two districts follow very different paths. District A is the quintessential marginal district. Since its creation in 1952 the district has sent an incumbent congressman down to defeat six times, all in general elections. Each party has won the seat with at least two different candidates during this period. No congressman has ever received as much as 58 percent of the vote, and the average winning percentage is a marginal 53+ percent of the vote. The district went Democratic in the 1964 Johnson landslide, but unlike many of his colleagues around the nation this Democratic congressman did not find himself in a safe district in 1966. On the contrary, he lost. But his replacement also failed to make district A safe. In the 1974 election, the Republican candidate won the district by only 5,000 votes out of more than 120,000 cast.

District B is another story. This district was created during the mid-forties. Between its creation and the 1964 election it chose two Republican congressmen, one for the great bulk of this time. But only during the Republican landslide of 1946 (which sent the famed—or notorious, depending on your

point of view—80th Congress to Washington) did the district give its winning congressional candidate a comfortable send-off. Between 1948 and
1962 the average winning percentage (always Republican) was a marginal
54+. As in district A, the Democrats captured district B in the 1964 landslide. But in contrast to district A, 1964 marked the death of a marginal in
district B. The Democratic congressman retained his seat in 1966, and in the
elections since he has managed an average victory percentage of more than 63
percent.

Why did the Democrat who took district A in 1964 not match the feat of his
counterpart in district B? And given that he did not, why has district A not
experienced a triumph of incumbency on the Republican side? One explanation we can eliminate is redistricting. District A underwent no boundary
change between 1952 and 1972 and then experienced a change amounting to
less than 5 percent of the district's population. The boundaries of district B
have not changed an iota since World War II. What then explains the electoral
differences between the two districts? Let us look more closely at district A.

During the 1950s both national and state candidates had family ties to the
district, ties that worked to Republican advantage in the former case and
Democratic advantage in the latter. Local observers agree that a portion of the
vote shifts that ended congressional careers during this period was completely
beyond the control of the congressmen or their challengers. A Republican
congressman captured the seat immediately following the Eisenhower era.
He was a conservative from the agricultural sector of the district, a somewhat
crusty personality of unquestioned integrity. The picture of this congressman
which emerges from my conversations is one of an officeholder who took
pride in his attendance record, perceived his job as the formulation of national
policy (often the obstruction of those doing the formulating), and, in general,
operated rather independently of his district. In 1964 local party officials
advised their candidates to dissociate themselves from the locally unpopular
Goldwater candidacy. The Republican conservative refused, saying that he
would not desert his friend Barry. When Lyndon Johnson improved on John
Kennedy's district showing by more than 30,000 votes, the Republican congressman followed his friend Barry into enforced retirement.

But the beneficiary of the Johnson landslide did not capitalize on his
opportunity. Instead, the freshman Democrat lost his seat in 1966, lost it in
fact to the conservative Republican he had defeated two years previously.
The Republican won several more terms, but the district remained in the
ranks of the marginals. In 1974 the congressman retired. The Republicans

held the seat, but only by the narrowest of margins. It came as a considerable surprise, then, when local observers assured me that the new Republican, a freshman with one year's experience, was safe, "unbeatable," that he "could hold the seat as long as he wants it." If these observers are correct (and they came from both parties), then another marginal has vanished.

How could this be? How could such a turnabout have occurred so quickly? Several explanations were offered to me. The freshman Republican has blanketed his district with communications. Both in terms of sheer volume and "effectiveness" he has greatly escalated the level of constituency contact maintained by his predecessor. Moreover, district observers believe that the freshman Republican's voting record is more closely attuned to his constituency than was that of his very conservative predecessor. The freshman voted to override a Ford veto or two, and he has supported certain federal programs which his predecessor consistently opposed. Several times I heard a remark to the effect that "he throws a few votes our (their) way now and then." Finally, the freshman Republican regularly returns to his district and travels from gathering to gathering saying:

> I'm your man in Washington. What are your problems? How can I help you?

While generally favorable to his successor, the former Republican congressman disapproves of the amount of time his successor spends in the district:

> How can he do his job in Washington when he's back here so much? People shouldn't expect a congressman to be running back home all the time.

In sum, a clear picture of district A emerges from my visit. During the 1950s this socioeconomically heterogeneous district was buffeted by broader political forces sufficiently powerful to tip the outcome of its congressional races. During the 1960s the district elected congressmen who apparently did not make all-out efforts to maximize their vote (more on the 1964 Democrat below). Now that someone is doing so, local observers and participants are betting another marginal has vanished.

What of district B? The picture of district B which emerges is that of a district ten years ahead of district A. Prior to 1964 the district was consistently but marginally Republican. The congressman who held the seat for most of this period was involved in controversial legislative battles such as Taft-

Hartley and Landrum-Griffin. He suffered politically from a personal problem, according to district contacts, and possibly more importantly from a political problem: declining Republican registration within the district. At the start of his tenure in Congress his party enjoyed a comfortable registration edge within the district. But this edge had dwindled by 1964, and today the parties are dead even. Some district politicians believe that the registration shift has little significance for national elections, that it is felt mostly on the local level. But it seems prudent to bear in mind that the triumph of incumbency in district B may reflect the changing political allegiances of the district. The defeated Republican congressman, naturally enough, is partial to this view.

Still, the Democrat who barely squeaked through in 1964 improved his margin in the Republican year of 1966 (when district Republicans fully expected to win) and has rolled up margins of 40,000 votes at times since—all this with a 50–50 split in registration. District observers agree that the strength of the congressman is bipartisan; a county chairman contends that in only one instance has any other national, state, or local candidate of either party run ahead of the Democratic congressman in the district or in the relevant common subarea of it. Can a registration shift from pro-Republican to dead even explain that kind of electoral muscle, especially when Republican turnout continues to remain generally higher than Democratic? Parenthetically, the registration shift appears to be home grown and not the result of changing composition of the district. A political reporter for the major district newspaper believes that the New Deal arrived more than half a generation late in district B. The district continues to be populated by the same kind of people. Only their registration has changed. I might also remark that registration in district A has shifted very little in recent years (Republicans have a slight edge). Any changes taking place there appear to be unrelated to registration.

Back to the point. Again, in district B we find a marked behavioral difference between the pre–1964 Republican congressman and the post–1964 Democratic congressman. Strictly speaking, the location of district B does not place it in a prime "Tuesday to Thursday club" area (East Coast areas so called because of the propensity of their congressman to put in a three-day week in Washington). In practice, however, the Democratic congressman is a member in good standing. By general agreement he is a pervasive presence in the district. He has no extensive campaign organization, although he maintains close ties with the regular party organizations in the three counties.

Primarily, however, the congressman relies on his own efforts, personally working the district at a feverish pace. A party chairman from a Republican area commented:

> Congressman (Democrat) comes to see people. Congressman (former Republican) didn't. The people know (Democrat). He's the first congressman to take an active interest in them.

The Democratic incumbent maintains three well-staffed offices in the district. These offices process a steady flow of constituency requests for aid in dealing with government agencies. Social security and veterans' matters are the most common kind of work handled. In this respect we find a difference between the Democratic incumbent and his principal Republican predecessor. The latter remarked:

> When I was in office I had four staff members. Now they have a regiment. That's just not necessary. It's a waste of the taxpayer's money, a frivolous expense.

The matter of the congressional staff is worthy of special notice. The retired Republican congressman in district A spontaneously brought it up. In discussing examples of the "hypocrisy" of modern Congressmen, the retiree pointed to the 1967 expansion of the congressional staff, a particularly heinous example in his view. He stated flatly:

> No congressman could possibly use sixteen staff members.

Necessity aside, the Democratic congressman in district B is using them (ten in his district), and they don't appear to be hurting him any. In fact, a principal campaign theme of this congressman has been (years before Jimmy Carter and Ronald Reagan):

> Send me to Washington. I will protect the little guy from the government.

No doubt he needs lots of staff to help him in his efforts.

Clearly, our two districts indicate that major changes in their congressional election patterns go hand in hand with behavioral changes on the part of the congressmen they elected, although the direction of causality is not yet clear. What might produce the kind of behavioral differences we observe between the pre-1964 Republican and the post-1964 Democrat in district B, and between the pre- and post-1974 Republicans in district A? The former Republican congressmen in the two districts lean toward the view that today's congressmen are of lower quality than the pre-1960 variety. Oversimplifying somewhat, in olden days strong men made up the Congress. The floor debates were something to behold. Giants walked on Capitol Hill. In those halcyon days legislators legislated. They concentrated more heavily on affairs of state than do their contemporary successors. They were motivated relatively more by the public interest and relatively less by reelection than today's congressmen.

A defeated Republican in district B, for example, remarks that in an era of $10,000 annual congressional salaries only two kinds of people were congressmen: those of independent means who did not need to be beholden to anyone and those who so loved public service they would not be beholden to anyone. He likens the lot of a 1940s congressman to that of a local school board member. There wasn't any money in it, so you only did it out of duty or love. As this congressman surveys the present scene he sees a Congress composed of 435 professional officeholders most of whom could not possibly earn $45,000 plus perks in the private sector. Perhaps he's right.

But political scientists are justifiably skeptical of theories which postulate that human nature has changed for the worse, that yesterday's political giants have given way to today's political pygmies. I will not contend that today's congressmen are more concerned with reelection than were their 1940s and 1950s predecessors. In all likelihood, since the New Deal era the average congressman's desire for reelection has remained constant. What has changed is the set of resources he possesses to invest in his reelection effort. Today's congressmen have more productive political strategies than previously. And these strategies are an unforeseen (at least by us) by-product of the growth of an activist federal government.

To elaborate, a plausible explanation of the political histories of our two cases looks rather simple. The changing nature of congressional elections in these two districts stems directly from the changing behavior of the congressmen who represented them. Both districts are heterogeneous in a socioeconomic sense and consequently in their basic political allegiances (for example, as illustrated by registration). So long as these districts are represented by congressmen who function principally as national policymakers (pre-1964 in district B, pre-1974 in district A), reasonably close congressional elections will naturally result. For every voter a congressman pleases by a policy stand he will displease someone else. The consequence is a marginal district. But if we have incumbents who deemphasize controversial policy positions and instead place heavy emphasis on nonpartisan, nonprogrammatic constituency service (for which demand grows as government expands), the resulting blurring of political friends and enemies is sufficient to shift the district out of the marginal camp. We do not need to postulate a congressman who is more interested in reelection today than previously. All we need postulate is a congressman sufficiently interested in reelection that he would rather be reelected as an errand boy than not be reelected at all.

The critical question is whether we can expand and flesh out the preceding explanation and use it to explain the national decline in marginal districts. I think we can.

The Washington establishment now lies before us.

Chapter 5
The Rise of the Washington Establishment

Dramatis Personae

I assume that most people most of the time act in their own self-interest. This is not to say that human beings seek only to amass tangible wealth but rather to say that human beings seek to achieve their own ends—tangible and intangible—rather than the ends of their fellow men. I do not condemn such behavior nor do I condone it (although I rather sympathize with Thoreau's comment that "if I knew for a certainty that a man was coming to my house with the conscious design of doing me good, I should run for my life").[1] I only claim that political and economic theories which presume self-interested behavior will prove to be more widely applicable than those which build on more altruistic assumptions.

What does the axiom imply when used in the specific context of this book, a context peopled by congressmen, bureaucrats, and voters? I assume that the primary goal of the typical congressman is reelection. Over and above the $57,000 salary plus "perks" and outside money, the office of congressman carries with it prestige, excitement, and power. It is a seat in the cockpit of government. But in order to retain the status, excitement, and power (not to mention more tangible things) of office, the congressman must win reelection every two years. Even those congressmen genuinely concerned with good public policy must achieve reelection in order to continue their work. Whether narrowly self-serving or more publicly oriented, the individual congressman finds reelection to be at least a necessary condition for the achievement of his goals.[2]

Moreover, there is a kind of natural selection process at work in the electoral arena. On average, those congressmen who are not primarily interested in reelection will not achieve reelection as often as those who are interested. We, the people, help to weed out congressmen whose primary motivation is not reelection. We admire politicians who courageously adopt the aloof role of the disinterested statesman, but we vote for those politicians who follow our wishes and do us favors.

What about the bureaucrats? A specification of their goals is somewhat

Distributed by Chicago Tribune-New York News Syndicate

more controversial—those who speak of appointed officials as public servants obviously take a more benign view than those who speak of them as bureaucrats. The literature provides ample justification for asserting that most bureaucrats wish to protect and nurture their agencies. The typical bureaucrat can be expected to seek to expand his agency in terms of personnel, budget, and mission. One's status in Washington (again, not to mention more tangible things) is roughly proportional to the importance of the operation one oversees. And the sheer size of the operation is taken to be a measure of importance. As with congressmen, the specified goals apply even to those bureaucrats who genuinely believe in their agency's mission. If they believe in the efficacy of their programs, they naturally wish to expand them and add new ones. All of this requires more money and more people. The genuinely committed bureaucrat is just as likely to seek to expand his agency as the proverbial empire-builder.[3]

And what of the third element in the equation, us? What do we, the voters who support the Washington system, strive for? Each of us wishes to receive a maximum of benefits from government for the minimum cost. This goal suggests maximum government efficiency, on the one hand, but it also suggests mutual exploitation on the other. Each of us favors an arrangement in which our fellow citizens pay for our benefits.

With these brief descriptions of the cast of characters in hand, let us proceed.

Tammany Hall Goes to Washington

What should we expect from a legislative body composed of individuals whose first priority is their continued tenure in office? We should expect, first, that the normal activities of its members are those calculated to enhance their chances of reelection. And we should expect, second, that the members would devise and maintain institutional arrangements which facilitate their electoral activities. These general propositions are the focus of the remainder of part 1 of this book.

For most of the twentieth century, congressmen have engaged in a mix of three kinds of activities: lawmaking, pork barreling, and casework. Congress is first and foremost a lawmaking body, at least according to constitutional theory. In every postwar session Congress "considers" thousands of bills and resolutions, many hundreds of which are brought to a record vote (over 500 in each chamber in the 93d Congress). Naturally the critical consideration in taking a position for the record is the maximization of approval in the home district. If the district is unaffected by and unconcerned with the matter at hand, the congressman may then take into account the general welfare of the country. (This sounds cynical, but remember that "profiles in courage" are sufficiently rare that their occurrence inspires books and articles.) Abetted by political scientists of the pluralist school, politicians have propounded an ideology which maintains that the good of the country on any given issue is simply what is best for a majority of congressional districts. This ideology provides a philosophical justification for what congressmen do while acting in their own self-interest.

A second activity favored by congressmen consists of efforts to bring home the bacon to their districts. Many popular articles have been written about the pork barrel, a term originally applied to rivers and harbors legislation but now generalized to cover all manner of federal largesse.[4] Congressmen consider new dams, federal buildings, sewage treatment plants, urban renewal projects, etc. as sweet plums to be plucked. Federal projects are highly visible, their economic impact is easily detected by constituents, and sometimes they even produce something of value to the district. The average constituent may have some trouble translating his congressman's vote on some civil rights issue into a change in his personal welfare. But the workers hired and supplies purchased in connection with a big federal project provide benefits that are widely appreciated. The historical importance congressmen attach to the pork barrel is reflected in the rules of the House. That body accords certain classes of legislation "privileged" status: they may come directly to the floor without passing through the Rules Committee, a traditional graveyard for legislation. What kinds of legislation are privileged? Taxing and spending bills, for one: the government's power to raise and spend money must be kept relatively unfettered. But in addition, the omnibus rivers and harbors bills of the Public Works Committee and public lands bills from the Interior Committee share privileged status. The House will allow a civil rights or defense procurement or environmental bill to languish in the Rules Committee, but it takes special precautions to insure that nothing slows down the approval of dams and irrigation projects.

A third major activity takes up perhaps as much time as the other two combined. Traditionally, constituents appeal to their Congressman for myriad favors and services. Sometimes only information is needed, but often constituents request that their congressman intervene in the internal workings of federal agencies to affect a decision in a favorable way, to reverse an adverse decision, or simply to speed up the glacial bureaucratic process. On the basis of extensive personal interviews with congressmen, Charles Clapp writes:

> Denied a favorable ruling by the bureaucracy on a matter of direct concern to him, puzzled or irked by delays in obtaining a decision,

confused by the administrative maze through which he is directed to proceed, or ignorant of whom to write, a constituent may turn to his congressman for help. These letters offer great potential for political benefit to the congressman since they affect the constituent personally. If the legislator can be of assistance, he may gain a firm ally; if he is indifferent, he may even lose votes.[5]

Actually congressmen are in an almost unique position in our system, a position shared only with high-level members of the executive branch. Congressmen possess the power to expedite and influence bureaucratic decisions. This capability flows directly from congressional control over what bureaucrats value most: higher budgets and new program authorizations. In a very real sense each congressman is a monopoly supplier of bureaucratic unsticking services for his district.

Every year the federal budget passes through the appropriations committees of Congress. Generally these committees make perfunctory cuts. But on occasion they vent displeasure on an agency and leave it bleeding all over the Capitol. The most extreme case of which I am aware came when the House committee took away the entire budget of the Division of Labor Standards in 1947 (some of the budget was restored elsewhere in the appropriations process). Deep and serious cuts are made occasionally, and the threat of such cuts keeps most agencies attentive to congressional wishes. Professors Richard Fenno and Aaron Wildavsky have provided extensive documentary and interview evidence of the great respect (and even terror) federal bureaucrats show for the House Appropriations Committee.[6] Moreover, the bureaucracy must keep coming back to Congress to have its old programs reauthorized and new ones added. Again, most such decisions are perfunctory, but exceptions are sufficiently frequent that bureaucrats do not forget the basis of their agencies' existence. For example, the Law Enforcement Assistance Administration (LEAA) and the Food Stamps Program had no easy time of it this last Congress (94th). The bureaucracy needs congressional approval in order to survive, let alone expand. Thus, when a congressman calls about some minor bureaucratic decision or regulation, the bureaucracy considers his accommodation a small price to pay for the goodwill its cooperation will produce, particularly if he has any connection to the substantive committee or the appropriations subcommittee to which it reports.

From the standpoint of capturing voters, the congressman's lawmaking activities differ in two important respects from his pork-barrel and casework activities. First, programmatic actions are inherently controversial. Unless his district is homogeneous, a congressman will find his district divided on many major issues. Thus when he casts a vote, introduces a piece of non-trivial legislation, or makes a speech with policy content he will displease some elements of his district. Some constituents may applaud the congressman's civil rights record, but others believe integration is going too fast. Some support foreign aid, while others believe it's money poured down a rathole. Some advocate economic equality, others stew over welfare cheaters. On such policy matters the congressman can expect to make friends as well as enemies. Presumably he will behave so as to maximize the excess of the former over the latter, but nevertheless a policy stand will generally make some enemies.

In contrast, the pork barrel and casework are relatively less controversial. New federal projects bring jobs, shiny new facilities, and general economic prosperity, or so people believe. Snipping ribbons at the dedication of a new post office or dam is a much more pleasant pursuit than disposing of a constitutional amendment on abortion. Republicans and Democrats, conservatives and liberals, all generally prefer a richer district to a poorer one. Of course, in recent years the river damming and stream-bed straightening activities of the Army Corps of Engineers have aroused some opposition among environmentalists. Congressmen happily reacted by absorbing the opposition and adding environmentalism to the pork barrel: water treatment plants are currently a hot congressional item.

Casework is even less controversial. Some poor, aggrieved constituent becomes enmeshed in the tentacles of an evil bureaucracy and calls upon Congressman St. George to do battle with the dragon. Again Clapp writes;

> A person who has a reasonable complaint or query is regarded as providing an opportunity rather than as adding an extra burden to an already busy office. The party affiliation of the individual even when known to be different from that of the congressman does not normally act as a deterrent to action. Some legislators have built their reputations and their majorities on a program of service to all constituents irrespective of party. Regularly, voters affiliated with the opposition in other contests lend strong support to the lawmaker whose intervention has helped them in their struggle with the bureaucracy.[7]

Even following the revelation of sexual improprieties, Wayne Hays won his Ohio Democratic primary by a two-to-one margin. According to a *Los An-*

geles Times feature story, Hays's constituency base was built on a foundation of personal service to constituents:

> They receive help in speeding up bureaucratic action on various kinds of federal assistance—black lung benefits to disabled miners and their families, Social Security payments, veterans' benefits and passports.
>
> Some constituents still tell with pleasure of how Hays stormed clear to the seventh floor of the State Department and into Secretary of State Dean Rusk's office to demand, successfully, the quick issuance of a passport to an Ohioan.[8]

Practicing politicians will tell you that word of mouth is still the most effective mode of communication. News of favors to constituents gets around and no doubt is embellished in the process.

In sum, when considering the benefits of his programmatic activities, the congressman must tote up gains and losses to arrive at a net profit. Pork barreling and casework, however, are basically pure profit.

A second way in which programmatic activities differ from casework and the pork barrel is the difficulty of assigning responsibility to the former as compared with the latter. No congressman can seriously claim that he is responsible for the 1964 Civil Rights Act, the ABM, or the 1972 Revenue Sharing Act. Most constituents do have some vague notion that their congressman is only one of hundreds and their senator one of an even hundred. Even committee chairmen have a difficult time claiming credit for a piece of major legislation, let alone a rank-and-file congressman. Ah, but casework, and the pork barrel. In dealing with the bureaucracy, the congressman is not merely one vote of 435. Rather, he is a nonpartisan power, someone whose phone calls snap an office to attention. He is not kept on hold. The constituent who receives aid believes that his congressman and his congressman alone got results. Similarly, congressmen find it easy to claim credit for federal projects awarded their districts. The congressman may have instigated the proposal for the project in the first place, issued regular progress reports, and ultimately announced the award through his office. Maybe he can't claim credit for the 1965 Voting Rights Act, but he can take credit for Littletown's spanking new sewage treatment plant.

Overall then, programmatic activities are dangerous (controversial), on the one hand, and programmatic accomplishments are difficult to claim credit for, on the other. While less exciting, casework and pork barreling are both safe and profitable. For a reelection-oriented congressman the choice is obvious.

The key to the rise of the Washington establishment (and the vanishing marginals) is the following observation: *the growth of an activist federal government has stimulated a change in the mix of congressional activities.* Specifically, a lesser proportion of congressional effort is now going into programmatic activities and a greater proportion into pork-barrel and case-work activities. As a result, today's congressmen make relatively fewer enemies and relatively more friends among the people of their districts.

To elaborate, a basic fact of life in twentieth-century America is the growth of the federal role and its attendant bureaucracy. Bureaucracy is the characteristic mode of delivering public goods and services. Ceteris paribus, the more the government attempts to do for people, the more extensive a bureaucracy it creates. As the scope of government expands, more and more citizens find themselves in direct contact with the federal government. Consider the rise in such contacts upon passage of the Social Security Act, work relief projects and other New Deal programs. Consider the millions of additional citizens touched by the veterans' programs of the postwar period. Consider the untold numbers whom the Great Society and its aftermath brought face to face with the federal government. In 1930 the federal bureaucracy was small and rather distant from the everyday concerns of Americans. By 1975 it was neither small nor distant.

As the years have passed, more and more citizens and groups have found themselves dealing with the federal bureaucracy. They may be seeking positive actions—eligibility for various benefits and awards of government grants. Or they may be seeking relief from the costs imposed by bureaucratic regulations—on working conditions, racial and sexual quotas, market restrictions, and numerous other subjects. While not malevolent, bureaucracies make mistakes, both of commission and omission, and normal attempts at redress often meet with unresponsiveness and inflexibility and sometimes seeming incorrigibility. Whatever the problem, the citizen's congressman is a source of succor. The greater the scope of government activity, the greater the demand for his services.

Private monopolists can regulate the demand for their product by raising or lowering the price. Congressmen have no such (legal) option. When the demand for their services rises, they have no real choice except to meet that demand—to supply more bureaucratic unsticking services—so long as they would rather be elected than unelected. This vulnerability to escalating constituency demands is largely academic, though. I seriously doubt that congressmen resist their gradual transformation from national legislators to errand boy-ombudsmen. As we have noted, casework is all profit. Congressmen have buried proposals to relieve the casework burden by establishing a national ombudsman or Congressman Reuss's proposed Administrative Counsel of the Congress. One of the congressmen interviewed by Clapp stated:

> Before I came to Washington I used to think that it might be nice if the individual states had administrative arms here that would take care of necessary liaison between citizens and the national government. But a congressman running for reelection is interested in building fences by providing personal services. The system is set to reelect incumbents regardless of party, and incumbents wouldn't dream of giving any of this service function away to any subagency. As an elected member I feel the same way.[9]

In fact, it is probable that at least some congressmen deliberately stimulate the demand for their bureaucratic fixit services. (See the exhibit at the end of this chapter). Recall that the new Republican in district A travels about his district saying:

> I'm your man in Washington. What are your problems? How can I help you?

And in district B, did the demand for the congressman's services rise so much between 1962 and 1964 that a "regiment" of constituency staff became necessary? Or, having access to the regiment, did the new Democrat stimulate the demand to which he would apply his regiment?

In addition to greatly increased casework, let us not forget that the growth of the federal role has also greatly expanded the federal pork barrel. The creative pork barreler need not limit himself to dams and post offices—rather old-fashioned interests. Today, creative congressmen can cadge LEAA money for the local police, urban renewal and housing money for local politicians, educational program grants for the local education bureaucracy. And there are sewage treatment plants, worker training and retraining programs, health services, and programs for the elderly. The pork barrel is full to overflowing. The conscientious congressman can stimulate applications for federal assistance (the sheer number of programs makes it difficult for local officials to stay current with the possibilities), put in a good word during consideration, and announce favorable decisions amid great fanfare.

In sum, everyday decisions by a large and growing federal bureaucracy bestow significant tangible benefits and impose significant tangible costs. Congressmen can affect these decisions. Ergo, the more decisions the bureaucracy has the opportunity to make, the more opportunities there are for the congressman to build up credits.

The nature of the Washington system is now quite clear. Congressmen (typically the majority Democrats) earn electoral credits by establishing various federal programs (the minority Republicans typically earn credits by fighting the good fight). The legislation is drafted in very general terms, so some agency, existing or newly established, must translate a vague policy mandate into a functioning program, a process that necessitates the promulgation of numerous rules and regulations and, incidentally, the trampling of numerous toes. At the next stage, aggrieved and/or hopeful constituents petition their congressman to intervene in the complex (or at least obscure) decision processes of the bureaucracy. The cycle closes when the congressman lends a sympathetic ear, piously denounces the evils of bureau-

Exhibit: How the Congressman-as-Ombudsman Drums up Business

NEED HELP WITH A FEDERAL PROBLEM?

Please feel free to communicate with me, in person, by phone or by mail. Daily from 9 a.m. until 5 p.m. my Congressional District office in Fullerton is open to serve you and your family. The staff will be able to help you with information or assistance on proposed Federal legislation and procedures of Federal agencies. If you are experiencing a problem with Social Security, educational assistance, Veterans Administration, Immigration, Internal Revenue Service, Postal Service, Environmental Protection Agency, Federal Energy Office or any other Federal agency, please contact me through this office. If you decide to write to me, please provide a telephone number as many times I can call you with information within a day or two.

CONGRESSMAN CHARLES E. WIGGINS
Brashears Center, Suite 103
1400 N. Harbor Boulevard
Fullerton, Ca 92635 (714) 870-7266

My Washington address is
Room 2445 Rayburn Building, Washington, D.C.
20515. Telephone (202) 225-4111.

U.S. House of Representatives
WASHINGTON D.C. 20515
PUBLIC DOCUMENT
OFFICIAL BUSINESS

Charles E. Wiggins M.C.

POSTAL CUSTOMER-LOCAL
39th District
CALIFORNIA

cracy, intervenes in the latter's decisions, and rides a grateful electorate to ever more impressive electoral showings. Congressmen take credit coming and going. They are the alpha and the omega.

The popular frustration with the permanent government in Washington is partly justified, but to a considerable degree it is misplaced resentment. *Congress is the linchpin of the Washington establishment.* The bureaucracy serves as a convenient lightning rod for public frustration and a convenient whipping boy for congressmen. But so long as the bureaucracy accommodates congressmen, the latter will oblige with ever larger budgets and grants of authority. Congress does not just react to big government—it creates it. All of Washington prospers. More and more bureaucrats promulgate more and more regulations and dispense more and more money. Fewer and fewer congressmen suffer electoral defeat. Elements of the electorate benefit from government programs, and all of the electorate is eligible for ombudsman services. But the general, long-term welfare of the United States is no more than an incidental by-product of the system.

Chapter 6

Back to the Vanishing Marginals: Some Loose Ends

As I suggested in the previous chapter, the marginals disappeared as the Washington system developed. Congressmen elected from marginal districts found it increasingly possible to base their reelection on their noncontroversial activities—their casework and success in procuring the pork—rather than on their lawmaking activities, which divided their districts. As Congress created a government ever larger and more far-reaching, it simultaneously increased the opportunities for its members to build up political credit with their constituents. In effect, I am proposing a behavioral change theory. Burnham, Erikson, and Ferejohn are correct: voting behavior in congressional elections has changed. But I think that the explanations of these authors are incomplete. Voting behavior did not change by itself. Rather, voting behavior changed in part because congressional behavior changed. Congressmen are not simply passive reactors to a changing electoral climate. They have helped to change that climate.

Several subsidiary questions still remain without satisfactory answers, however. In this short chapter I would like to address three of them. First, what is the exact nature of the congressional incumbency effect? Second, are the hypothesized changes in congressional behavior sufficiently large to account for the vanishing marginals? Third, what about the timing of the electoral shift, its abrupt nature?

The Nature of the Incumbency Effect

If an increasing number of congressmen are devoting increasing resources to constituency service, then we would expect that increasing numbers of voters must think of their congressmen less as policymakers than as ombudsmen and pork barrelers. If so, other implications are immediate. First, party identification will be less influential in determining the congressional vote, not just because of the unusual national politics of the later 1960s, but because *objectively* the congressman is no longer as policy relevant as he once was. In legislative matters he is merely one vote of 435. But in bureaucratic matters he is a benevolent, nonpartisan power. And if more and more citizens come to think of their congressmen in this manner, then the basis of the incumbency effect is obvious. *Experience in Washington and congressional seniority count when dealing with the bureaucracy.* So long as the incumbent can elude a personal morality rap and refrain from casting outlandish votes, he is naturally preferred over a newcomer. *This incumbency effect is not only understandable; it is rational.* And it would grow over time as increasing numbers of citizens come to regard their congressman as a troubleshooter in the Washington bureaucracies.

Recall the troublesome table 3 from chapter 3. Some draw the seemingly reasonable conclusion that the incumbency effect is unrelated to the communications incumbents shower on their constituents, because the informational advantage incumbents possess did not increase between 1958 and 1974, while the incumbency advantage apparently increased during this period. But what if the *content* of the information has changed over time? What if in 1958 those voters who had heard or read something about the incumbent had heard or read about one or more of his policy stands, whereas in 1970 they had heard or read about his effectiveness in getting Vietnam veterans' checks in the mail? Some voters will agree with the policy stand, others will disagree, but everyone will applaud efforts in behalf of the veterans. Even if the proportion aware of the incumbent has stayed constant around 50 percent, one would expect him to capture a larger chunk of that 50 percent if his constituents' knowledge relates to his casework and pork-barrel activities rather than to his policy positions. Thus an increasing incumbency advantage is quite consistent with a constant informational advantage if information about the incumbent has grown increasingly noncontroversial in content and correspondingly positive in its impact.

Furthermore, as suggested above, if popular perceptions of the congressman gradually change from national legislator to district ombudsman, even those citizens having no specific information about incumbent or challenger act quite sensibly in going with the candidate who has experience and seniority.

Thus there are good reasons to anticipate an incumbency effect both among those with specific political information about the incumbent and among those without such information. Moreover, that effect is not an irrational response to a familiar name; rather, it is a justifiable response to a changed political reality.

The Magnitude of the Incumbency Effect

Some of my colleagues have conceded that the trends I have hypothesized probably are occurring but have expressed doubt that the magnitude of the behavioral changes could account for the decline of the marginals. A congressman would have to do one hell of a lot of personal favors, they say. And congressmen still seem to spend some time passing laws.

For clarity's sake I have presented my arguments in bold outline. But in order to account for the decline of the marginals we do *not* need to claim that *all* congressmen have opted exclusively for an ombudsman role and that *all* constituents now think of their congressman in nonprogrammatic terms. In actuality, the disappearance of a marginal requires only marginal (no pun intended) change. To illustrate, let us take Mayhew's bimodal vote distribution for 1972 and take away Erikson's estimated 5 percent incumbency effect. That is, we assume that no incumbency effect exists, so 5 percent is subtracted from the vote of each incumbent running in 1972. Figures 3a and 3b compare the 1972 vote distribution with the hypothetical deflated one.

The large difference between the distributions even surprised me when I performed the calculations. Just taking away a 5 percent incumbency effect wipes out the trough in the middle range of the actual vote distribution. Subtracting a hypothetical *10 percent* effect returns the distribution to the 1948 appearance. The conclusion seems obvious. To explain the vanishing marginals we need only argue that over the past quarter of a century expanded constituency service and pork-barrel opportunities have given the marginal

Figure 3a. Congressional Vote in Districts with Incumbents Running, 1972

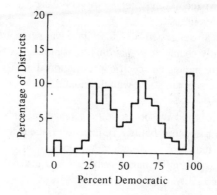

Figure 3b. Congressional Vote in Districts with Incumbents Running Minus 5 Percent Incumbency Advantage, 1972

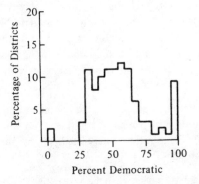

congressman the opportunity to switch 3–5 percent of those who would otherwise oppose him on policy grounds to his supporting coalition. Considering the magnitude of the growth in the federal role during that same period, such a shift seems eminently plausible.

The Timing of the Changes

The growth of the federal role has been reasonably continuous albeit with definite take-off points such as the New Deal and World War II. The decline of congressional competition, in contrast, has been somewhat more erratic. No change was noticeable before the 1950s, and the most pronounced change appears to have occurred over a relatively short period during the mid-sixties. How do we reconcile the differences in the two trends?

One would expect some lag between the onset of bureaucratic expansion and the decline of the marginals, because congressmen presumably would not grasp the new opportunities immediately. Moreover, the effects of federal expansion are cumulative. In the early part of the postwar period congressmen may have used their opportunities to the fullest, but the electoral impact might have been imperceptible. By the 1960s, however, constituency service opportunities had cumulated to a significant electoral factor.

Still, the mid-sixties decline is especially pronounced. I think it is probably too much to argue that Great Society programs translated into casework and then votes quite so immediately. But one possible explanation of the sixties decline lies in recent work by Professor Richard Fenno.[1] Fenno attaches great importance to a congressman's "home style," his basic patterns of interaction with his district. Home style includes three components: (1) the congressman's allocation of time, effort, and staff to his district, (2) his personal style, and (3) his explanation for his Washington activities. Most relevant for my discussion are Fenno's observations about the constraints imposed by home styles. Fenno argues that congressional careers pass through two stages, expansionist and protectionist, and

> Once in the protectionist phase . . . the dominant impulse is conservative. Keep the support you had "last time"; do what you did "last time." The tendency to follow established patterns, to observe stylistic constraints, is strong.[2]

Now when one considers that between the 88th and 90th Congress (1963–67) one third of the membership of the House changed, a plausible hypothesis emerges. The new representatives placed greater emphasis on constituency service than did those whom they replaced. The average freshman in 1965 replaced a congressman elected in 1952 or 1954. The latter had formed their home styles in a different era. Moreover, particularly in 1964 many of the freshmen were Democrats who had won election in heretofore Republican districts. They can hardly be blamed for assuming that they could not win reelection on policy grounds. They had every incentive to adopt home styles that emphasized nonprogrammatic constituency service. (And, I might add, if they were not smart enough to see that themselves, it was pointed out to them. The congressional party leadership, assisted by the American Political Science Association, emphasized the importance of constituency service during the 1964 orientation sessions!) I might also point out that the Democrats who won district A in 1964 and lost it in 1966 did not follow the good advice offered him. According to local supporters, he was seldom heard from, even during the 1966 campaign. He became totally engrossed in his Washington affairs.

Paradoxically, then, the electoral upheavals of the 1960s may have produced the electoral stability of the early 1970s. New congressmen chose home styles best adapted to the changed congressional environment. Is it purely coincidence that these fresh Congresses have raised personal staff allotments by over 50 percent since 1967? (More on this in chapter 7.)

Chapter 7
Some Circumstantial Evidence Surrounding the Rise of the Washington Establishment

In chapter 5 I discussed the kinds of activities favored by congressmen oriented toward reelection and how the mix of those activities has changed as the federal government has grown. The discussion was relatively theoretical. Congressmen, after all, do not keep public records of the time they spend in various activities. In this chapter I will discuss several ways in which congressmen have altered their institutional surroundings in order to facilitate the performance of electorally profitable activities. In this area more evidence is available, although it is of a circumstantial nature. It takes on significance when examined in light of the previously developed argument.

During the past twenty years, congressional incumbents have adopted various plans to increase the resources available for investment in their reelection efforts and to modify existing institutional arrangements to better serve their electoral ends. One highly visible change is the doubling of their personal staffs. A second is the continual increase in various congressional "perks." A third, more far-reaching change, is the devolution of congressional power from full committee to subcommittee level, thereby giving rank-and-file congressmen a bigger piece of the action and producing a proliferation of "subgovernments" in Washington. Finally, I will discuss the creation of formal legislative liaison offices in the bureaucracy, an executive innovation which incumbent congressmen have used to good advantage.

The Congressional Staff

Sad to say, the subject of the congressional staff is largely neglected. The few published studies by political scientists deal with committee staffs, the professional and clerical employees of the standing committees. My concern is with the personal staffs of congressmen. Recall from chapter 4 how a defeated congressman complained that compared to his former staff the present Democratic incumbent had a "regiment." The former congressman's observation is a legitimate one. Office staff authorizations are stated in terms of both a maximum number of employees and a maximum base payroll. The story of both in the past twenty years has been quite simple: steady expansion.

In the early 1960s, before the disappearance of the marginals became apparent, each member of the House was authorized to hire up to nine staff at a basic total payroll of some $20,000, a number in practice augmented to about $50,000 by numerous pay raise enactments. During the 1960s the authorization crept up to eleven, then to fifteen by 1971 at a total payroll of more than $141,000. (Members who had heavily populated districts—over 500,000—were allowed one extra employee during this period.) Today (1977) congressmen are allowed up to eighteen staff on a total payroll of more than $225,000. Thus we have seen a doubling of personal staff resources during the past fifteen years, most of which occurred at the same time the marginal districts were disappearing. In the Senate, staff sizes are tied to state population, but there too the story is the same: rapid expansion. Currently senators receive between $400,000 and $800,000 annually to hire personal staff, plus an extra $100,000 for three staff earmarked to aid with committee work.

Table 5 details some features of the congressional staff at three points in time: prior to the decline of the marginals and the staff expansions of the 1960s, while both were occurring, and following the decline in the marginals and the doubling of the staffs. The simple increase in the number of authorized staff is clearly apparent, from 2,300 in 1960 to more than 5,000 in 1974.

Table 5. Growth of Personal Staffs of Congressmen, 1960–74

	1960	1967	1974
Total staff	2,344	3,276	5,109
Percentage of total staff assigned to district offices	14%	26%	34%
Percentage of congressmen whose district offices open only when congressman is home or after adjournment	29%	11%	2%
Percentage of congressmen listing multiple district offices	4%	18%	47%

Source: *Annual Congressional Staff Directories,* compiled by Charles B. Brownson.

Rather more interesting are the other three pieces of data. First, the percent of staff assigned to the home districts has more than doubled, from 14 percent of all listed staff members in 1960 to 34 percent in 1974. Second, congressional staff operations in the district are now permanent operations. In 1960 nearly 30 percent of all congressmen specified that their district offices were open only when they were home or after the adjournment of Congress. Today one can find only slight traces of intermittent staff operations.[1] Third, district staff offices as well as district staff have increased. In 1960 only 4 percent of all congressmen listed more than one district office (generally two; only one congressman listed three). But by the mid-seventies we see that multiple offices are the case as often as not.

What are the duties of these growing numbers of congressional staff? Unfortunately, the little data available are both extremely fragmentary and rather dated. The occasional academic writings on the subject tend to rely on the same sketchy figures, so I have little choice but to do likewise. A mid-sixties survey of congressional staffs produced the data summarized in table 6.

If these data are representative, then members of the House spend nearly 30 percent of their time on constituency service, while their staffs spend well over half their time on such matters. (Bear in mind too that some legislative

Table 6. Average Washington Work Week of Congressman and Personal Staff

Function	Congressman	Personal Staff
Legislative	65%	14%
Constituency service	28	25
Education/publicity	8	10
Correspondence (mix of constituency service and education)	–	41
Other	–	10

Source: Adapted from John Saloma, Congress and the New Politics (Boston: Little, Brown, 1969), Tables 6.5 and 6.7, pp. 184–85. Data on congressional work week based on returns from 150 offices, on staff work week from 60 offices.

matters are directly constituency related—authorization of various district projects, for example.) If anything, the data may understate the constituency service function. Congressional scholar Kenneth Olson, who has studied the casework load, estimates that

> the chances are good that an analysis of the total time expended by members and their staffs on all congressional work would find casework the leading activity.[2]

Moreover, the data in the table should be read in the light of two additional considerations. First, the casework load no doubt has increased since the data were gathered in 1965. Even if congressmen did not consciously try to expand the casework burden, the increase in federal programs over the last ten years surely has stimulated a large number of additional requests. Second, the data in table 6 refer to the work week of the *Washington* office. Presumably the *district* offices are totally absorbed in constituency service. Thus the expansion in the district staff operations documented in table 5 represents almost entirely increases in constituency services.

There is an ironic twist to the story of the congressional staff expansions. Of all the possible changes (''reforms'') that various observers have urged upon Congress during the postwar period, staff increases are perhaps the least controversial. Congressional actions to augment staff numbers and quality are almost universally encouraged and applauded. The reason is a naïve assumption about the purposes to which congressmen put their staffs. Reformers correctly see that the world has grown much more complex in recent years, that policy matters now require more than the commonsense of the ''man from Missouri.'' Economic, technological, and social scientific expertise is critically important for making effective public policy decisions. The executive is well endowed with such expertise, but for years congressmen plodded along with a clerk and a secretary. To reformers, a large professional staff is just the thing to assure better public policies and a more even balance between Congress and the executive branch.

But in reality what are the uses to which congressmen put their staffs? Improved public policy is a goal that most congressmen favor. But reelection is certainly a more important goal. And when given sixteen or eighteen employees to allocate as they see fit, congressmen quite naturally put the lion's share to work on the most important thing, reelection, while perhaps reserving a few for secondary matters such as formulating our country's laws and programs.

Other Perquisites of Office

When public interest groups criticize the advantages of incumbency, they generally are referring to a variety of tangible resources freely available to incumbents but not to their challengers. In addition to the well-known congressional frank, congressmen receive allowances for postage (airmail and special delivery), stationery and office supplies, telephone and telegraph use, and travel to their home districts. When we look at any of these allowances over the period of our study, the story is the expected one: they go up.[3]

Naturally we expect some increase in the various allowances. Inflation has steadily pushed up the price of stationery, air fares, and office rental. And, of course, postal rates have increased. But Congress has more than kept up with inflation. The 1965 increase in office rental allowances, for example, also included authorization for more district offices. The increases documented in row four of table 5 reflect more than just keeping up with inflation.

The case of travel allowances is no doubt the most interesting. In the early 1960s, before the noticeable drop in the number of marginal districts, members of the House and Senate were authorized to make three expense-paid round trips home each year. By 1966 the Senate had increased the authorization to six per year, while the House had upped it to five. By 1968 congressmen were allowed one trip for each month the Congress was in session, for a maximum of twelve per year, while senators were authorized a flat twelve per year. By 1973 representatives were up to eighteen trips per year. At present congressmen are entitled to twenty-six trips home per year, while senators receive forty-two to forty-six. (House and Senate *staff* also have received increasing authorization for trips to the district or state.)

Congressmen are going home more, pressing the flesh, getting around. They are building a personal base of support, one dependent on personal contacts and favors. The greatly increased presence of the congressman in his district dovetails nicely with the greatly enlarged district staff operations. The travel increases also suggest a tentative answer to a question some might raise about the staff increases. To wit, are congressmen just as devoted to lawmaking activities now as ever? Have they increased the staff in order to relieve themselves of the casework burden? I don't think so.

First, the enlarged staff requires supervision; it doesn't run itself. Second, even if a constant proportion of the increased casework was "bucked" up to the congressman for his personal attention now as previously, this would still be a major increase in casework requiring his personal intervention. And, most importantly, in the two districts which I have examined closely increased attention to casework and constituency problems generally goes hand in hand with frequent presence in the district:

> How can he do his job in Washington when he's back here so much? People shouldn't expect a congressman to be running back home all the time.

The greatly increased congressional travel allowances suggest that my two cases are not exceptions. In all likelihood, both the staff and the congressman are devoting a greater proportion of their time to constituency service now than they were in the early 1960s.

In the aftermath of the Wayne Hays imbroglio the House of Representatives has taken some action to "reform" the use of special allowances. No longer are congressmen permitted to withdraw stationery or postal allowances in cash, for example. And reporting requirements have been tightened. But the reforms contain a sweetener for incumbents as well. No longer are the allowances kept separate. Now members of the House have one general fund which they can allocate as they see fit; telephone money can be used for travel, etc. They've given themselves a bit more flexibility.

In 1964, prior to the occurrence of much that has just been described, Representative Michael Kirwan (D., Ohio) wrote candidly:

> No congressman who gets elected and who minds his business should ever be beaten. Everything is there for him to use if he'll only keep his nose to the grindstone and use what is offered.[4]

The changes that have occurred since the time of Kirwan's comment only reinforce its basic accuracy.

The Continued Decentralization of Congressional Power

In chapter 1, I remarked that curbs on the arbitrary powers of the congressional party leadership at the beginning of this century were a natural outgrowth of the increasing professionalization of congressmen. With more and more congressmen wishing to retain their seats for long periods, iron party discipline became intolerable. The individual congressman desired the flexibility to follow the wishes of his district when party-district conflicts arose. Moreover, taking power from the hands of the party leadership and spreading it more widely around the chamber gave individual members a greater opportunity to take actions to enhance their reelection efforts. The seniority system was the natural response to a group of budding career congressmen. Power was distributed more widely to a larger group of standing committee chairmen (there were about sixty standing committees in 1910), who would attain their positions by the automatic workings of the seniority system. Acceptance of the seniority system gave local districts the upper hand over the national parties in the U.S. Congress.

The distribution of power within Congress remained relatively constant throughout the mid-century period, but in recent years the trend toward further decentralization rapidly picked up speed. The development of the congressional subcommittee system is the most obvious indicator.

In 1946 the Legislative Reorganization Act rationalized an overgrown, outdated full committee structure. On the face of it, the reorganization (cutting by more than half the number of standing committees) was a major centralization of formal authority. But the proliferation of subcommittees soon began to offset the major thrust of the reorganization. Since 1946 the number of full committees has increased by only one in the House and three in the Senate, but table 7 details the steady growth of subcommittees. Bear in mind that in 1973, 243 majority Democrats sat in the House, while 59 sat in the Senate. On average, one of every two Democrats in the House was chairman of a subcommittee, while every Senate Democrat chaired an average of two subcommittees.

Not only has the number of subcommittees undergone a dramatic increase, but their powers and autonomy also have increased in the wake of changes (called "reforms," of course) that occurred in the House in the early

Table 7. Growth of Congressional Subcommittee System

Year	House	Senate
1955	83	79
1963	113	90
1973	125	128

Key: Table entries are number of subcommittees of congressional standing committees.

Source: Adapted from table 5 of Norman Ornstein and David Rohde, "Seniority and Future Power in Congress," in Norman Ornstein, ed., *Change in Congress* (New York: Praeger, 1975), pp. 72–87.

1970s.[5] First, in 1971 members were limited to the chairmanship of one subcommittee. Senior members who were hoarding chairmanships were forced to relinquish them to less senior members. Later, in 1973, a subcommittee "bill of rights" further reinforced the devolution of power. No longer could full committee chairmen arbitrarily designate subcommittee chairmen; full committee or subcommittee seniority (depending on the wishes of the committee Democrats) would henceforth determine subcommittee chairmanships. Subcommittee jurisdictions were fixed; full committee chairmen no longer could establish vague subcommittee jurisdictions in order to maximize their own flexibility in assigning legislation. Subcommittees were guaranteed adequate budgets and staffing; no longer could a full committee chairman starve a subcommittee or pack its staff with his minions. The full impact of these changes has yet to be determined, but it is clear that twenty-odd full committee chairmen have been weakened and 120-odd subcommittee chairmen strengthened. Congress now has a surfeit of chiefs and a shortage of Indians.

But aren't such reforms democratic (small *d*), one might ask? And isn't democracy good in itself? Perhaps, but democracy has its cost. In particular, those who applaud internal democratic reforms should not criticize Congress for inefficiency, shortsightedness, and footdragging. For example, public interest groups applaud the democratization of Congress, on the one hand, and deplore Congress's failure to formulate a national energy policy, on the other. There is something of an inconsistency here. How many are aware that in 1976 eleven subcommittees from six standing committees had a legitimate claim to a piece of the action in the energy area? These were:

1. Conservation, Energy and National Resources, chaired by Moorhead of Pennsylvania (Government Operations)
2. Water and Power Resources, chaired by Johnson of California ⎫
3. Energy and the Environment, chaired by Udall of Arizona ⎬ All of Interior and Insular Affairs
4. Mines and Mining, chaired by Mink of Hawaii ⎭
5. Energy and Power, chaired by Dingell of Michigan ⎫
6. Health and the Environment, chaired by Rogers of Florida ⎬ Both of Interstate and Foreign Commerce

7. Fisheries and Wildlife Conservation and the Environment, chaired
   by Leggett of California (Merchant Marines and Fisheries)
8. Water Resources, chaired by Roberts of Texas (Public Works)
9. Energy Research, Development and
   Demonstration, (Fossil Fuels) chaired
   by Hechler of West Virginia   All of Science
10. Energy Research, Development and   and Technol-
    Demonstration, chaired by McCormack   ogy
    of Washington
11. Environment and the Atmosphere,
    chaired by Brown of California

(Additionally, various Appropriations subcommittees get their thumbs in
the pie at that stage of the process.)

Each of these subcommittees can lay claim to some piece of any energy-
environment policy decision. And given the political incentive to claim credit, most of them will do so. Moreover, compound the above division of
responsibility by adding the equally elaborate one that exists in the Senate.
The result is more than twenty congressional power bases for senators to
advertise presidential hopes, congressmen to advertise senatorial hopes,
and/or everyone to advertise reelection hopes. This is democracy in action?

   Political scientists and political observers foreshadowed the rise of the
Washington establishment when they wrote of "subgovernments" (jour-
nalist Douglas Cater's term), "whirlpools" (Professor Ernest Griffith's
term), and "policy systems" (Professors Eugene Eidenberg's and Roy Morey's term).[6] Professor Randall Ripley writes:

> Most of the interaction between Congress and the bureaucracy repre-
> sents the ongoing activities of subgovernments. The basic institutional
> units in typical interaction are standing subcommittees (occasionally a
> full committee) from the House or Senate and various administrative
> units below the departmental level in the executive branch such as
> bureaus, agencies, services, and administrations. Much of the detailed
> business of the government is carried on between these units, some-
> times with the participation of interest group representatives. Larger
> units (for example, the entire House or Senate, the White House, or the
> office of a departmental secretary) get involved in details much less
> frequently. In general, only highly visible and politically sensitive

issues are likely to receive attention from the larger units; relatively less visible matters are often handled completely by a bureau speaking for the entire executive branch and a subcommittee speaking for the entire House and Senate. Individual members of the House and Senate and their staff members also get involved with the bureaucracy, usually because of a pending "case" involving a constituent.[7]

In other words, political observers are aware that cozy little groups of congressmen, bureaucrats, and interest group representatives make numerous day-to-day policy decisions. What has been less obvious is the manner in which the number of these subgovernments has been proliferating as the power of the twenty-odd full committees has been dispersed among the 120-odd subcommittees. If they so desire, most congressmen now have the opportunity to head up a subgovernment. By protecting a few agencies under their jurisdiction and accommodating a few concerned interest groups, the congressman buys electoral credit from the latter and wields influence over the former.

Two other facts of congressional life reinforce the usefulness (from the standpoint of individual congressmen) of this system of divided-up government. First, most congressmen gravitate to those committees which enable them to satisfy their reelection goal.[8] Oversimplifying, Westerners head for Interior, rural congressmen for Agriculture, inner city congressmen for Judiciary, and so forth. (The few generalized power committees—Appropriations, Ways and Means, Rules—stand astride the legislative process at so many points that their members can trade influence with members of all the standing committees.) Thus congressmen eventually gain influence in those subgovernments of particular concern to them and, by implication, their districts. Their power in the subgovernment translates directly into electoral credit for favorable policy decisions and successful intervention in the bureaucracy.

A second, related fact is congressional observance of reciprocity: "You scratch my back, and I'll scratch yours," or "Keep your nose out of my business, and I'll reciprocate." Given that most congressmen end up in the subgovernments of particular concern to them, observance of reciprocity is not very costly in terms of lost opportunities, and it is very profitable in terms of unfettered influence in an area vital to their continued reelection.

In sum, the decentralization of congressional power has created numerous subgovernments that enable individual members to control policy decisions and influence elements of the bureaucracy which are of particular concern to their districts. Increased electoral security is the natural result. On the face of it, the system is highly democratic. But do numerous piecemeal, uncoordinated decisions motivated primarily by congressional desire for reelection add up to good public policy? Advocates of ever more democracy might well consider this question.

The Growth of Legislative Liaison

American reformers show a great fondness for tinkering with the formal rules and procedures of the political system. Too often they naïvely assume that a simple rules change will solve a problem or alleviate an undesirable situation. Too seldom do they attempt an in-depth analysis of why the problem exists. Who profits from the existing state of affairs? Who stands to lose by changes in the status quo? As a result of incomplete analyses, procedural reforms often turn out to have unanticipated consequences. Regulatory commissions protect the regulated and exploit the public. Campaign spending limits work against congressional challengers. Opening up the primary process comes uncomfortably close to giving us Hubert Humphrey in a brokered convention. And congressional staff increases make incumbents ever more secure.

In this section I wish to suggest how congressman have taken advantage of an executive innovation, an innovation probably intended to take advantage of them. The institutional innovation to which I refer is the establishment of formal legislative liaison offices within the cabinet departments of the national government. The Defense and State departments established such offices in the late 1940s. The Post Office, Commerce, and HEW followed by 1955. In the early years of the Kennedy administration, under the direction of Larry O'Brien, the establishment of liaison offices was completed.[9] Existing liaison offices also were expanded. Again, data are fragmentary, but the data in table 8 on the expansion of the Defense Liaison Office are suggestive of the mid-sixties growth.

Prior to the creation of formal offices of legislative liaison, relations between Congress and the bureaucracy took place primarily at the bureau level. Congressmen had to develop their own personal contacts on the basis of interactions in the policy-making and appropriations processes. But with the

Table 8. Growth of Legislative Liaison Personnel, Department of Defense

	1963	1965
Office of the Secretary	13	34
Army	48	92
Air Force	119	144
Navy	50	70
Total	230	340

Source: G. Russell Pipe, "Congressional Liaison: The Executive Branch Consolidates Its Relations with Congress," *Public Administration Review* 26 (1966): 14–24.

establishment of formal liaison operations (centered in the office of the cabinet secretary) congressmen gained a direct line from the top into the bureaucracy.

In theory the establishment of liaison offices would help the executive branch to lead Congress, to coordinate the decentralized power centers in that body, to show parochial committee barons why they should not amend a presidential initiative umpteen ways to Sunday. In practice, however, liaison officers are a hot line into their respective departments. A small favor for a congressman's constituent? Sure, it's a cheap price to pay for his goodwill on a legislative proposal dear to the department's heart. Washington attorney and writer Edward de Grazia recognizes and approves of this turn of affairs:

> liaison with key members of the executive branch appears to give the congressman (1) direct access to those who make executive policy— high-ranking officials in the secretaries' offices; (2) a "point of view" concerning departmental administration; (3) information about policy questions, to fill what sometimes seems "a vacuum"; and (4) *perhaps most importantly, assistance in the meeting of constituent needs.* (My emphasis)[10]

What kinds of assistance do the liaison offices provide congressmen? De Grazia offers the example of the Agency for International Development:

A sampling which represented probably 75 percent of the total, was made of matters handled in the AID Congressional Liaison Office during a single week. The sampling revealed 168 telephone calls from members of Congress and their staffs on such matters as: a company in Wisconsin wanting to bid on planes; a constituent wanting an appointment on a project in Guatemala; a company in North Dakota wanting a contract; a firm protesting an AID contract award to an Oregon firm; another inquiry on behalf of the Oregon firm; the faculty at Roberts College in Turkey complaining about AID clearance requirements; the population problem; Vietnam; housing guaranties; an OAS conference; aid to Yugoslavia; AID-financed procurements in the United States; balance of payments and gold flow; Cooley loans; and employment interest of constituents. During that week there were also 84 requests from members of Congress for information; the appropriate materials were assembled and sent out by the Congressional Liaison staff. Calls or visits were made by the staff to 71 senators and congressmen for the purpose of assisting them, at their request, with various AID questions and problems. Approximately 75 letters were sent during that week to members of Congress in response to mail or telephone requests.[11]

And certainly it is doubtful that AID interests congressmen nearly as much as HEW, HUD, the Department of Agriculture, the Social Security Administration, or the Veterans Administration.

A fine example of congressional ingenuity comes from a short case study by Professor Randall Ripley of the congressional battle over the debt limit in 1963. Writes Ripley:

On Friday, May 10, McCormack, Albert, John Moss (the deputy whip), and Mills met Lawrence O'Brien, chief of White House congressional liaison, three O'Brien assistants, the administrative assistant to the whip, and the Assistant Secretary of the Treasury for congressional liaison. Mills reviewed a list of all Democrats and announced their reported position on the bill. When a member was announced as doubtful or against the bill, the Speaker or Majority Leader called him immediately and urged him to support it. Likewise, when a member favoring the bill was reported as planning to be absent, the Speaker called him and asked him to stay. One member who was asked to cancel a trip abroad (which he did) *used the occasion to arrange an appointment with O'Brien for himself and another Demo-*

crat to talk about a proposed veterans hospital consolidation in their districts (my emphasis).[12]

Here is a neat instance of the Washington system in operation. Congressmen agree to go along with some executive desire if the price is right, the executive branch gets the support it needs, constituents see evidence of the power of their congressmen, and the latter increase their margins at the polls. Was the increase in the debt limit good policy? Who knows? Who cares?

Chapter 8
Alternative Views

In discussing the concept of a Washington establishment two distinct types of questions arise. First, does one exist, and, if so, what exactly is it? Second, is the system undesirable, and should it be changed? I have argued in the preceding pages that there is an identifiable Washington system, composed of Congress and the federal bureaucracies operating in a seemingly antagonistic but fundamentally symbiotic relationship. To recount briefly, by working to establish various federal programs (or in some cases fighting their establishment) congressmen earn electoral credit from concerned elements of their districts. Some federal agency then takes Congress's vague policy mandate and makes the detailed decisions necessary to translate the legislation into operating programs. The implementation and operation of the programs by the agencies irritate some constituents and suggest opportunities for profit to others. These aggrieved and/or hopeful constituents then appeal to their congressman to intervene in their behalf with the bureaucratic powers that be. The system is connected when congressmen decry bureaucratic excesses and red tape while riding a grateful electorate to ever more impressive electoral showings.

Thus congressmen appropriate all the public credit generated in the system, while the bureaucracy absorbs all the costs. The bureaucrats may not enjoy their status as objects of public opprobrium, but so long as they accommodate congressmen larger budgets and grants of authority will be forthcoming. All of Washington prospers as ever larger cadres of bureaucrats promulgate ever more numerous regulations and spend ever more money. Meanwhile, ever fewer congressmen meet electoral defeat. This is the Washington system.

What should we think of such a system, beyond the trace of disillusionment we always feel upon finding that childhood ideals are not reflected in political reality? There are three recognizably distinct reactions to my description of the Washington system: (1) the cynical reaction that runs through the pages of this book, (2) a more optimistic reaction that looks at the bright side of the system, (3) an alarmist reaction that holds that the Washington system will evolve into something worse. Let us take these in order.

The Cynical View

Congressmen actively exploit the bureaucracy and the citizenry. The bureaucracy passively exploits Congress and the people. And the people? They are put in a position of attempting futilely to exploit each other. There is a difference between exchange and exploitation. People do receive services from their congressmen, and in return they provide votes. But when grateful constituents reelect their congressmen, they fail to realize that they are helping to perpetuate a system which subordinates the content of public policy to the desires of congressmen to obtain special credits with which to impress their districts. (More on this below.)

The recent campaigns provide indications that the exploitive character of the Washington system is becoming recognized. First, increasing numbers of citizens have turned to ''outsider'' political candidates. These citizens are only vaguely aware of what is wrong, but increasingly they feel that something is and that the source of the problem is Washington, D.C. Second, consider the suspicion and/or opposition of the ''liberal establishment'' to such candidates as Jimmy Carter, Jerry Brown, and other new Democrats. The liberal establishment is a subset of the Washington establishment (as is the conservative establishment, to some extent). In addition to liberal bureaucrats themselves, private consultants, faculty members at prestigious eastern universities, innumerable lawyers, and their associates in the media all fatten off the Washington system. Threats to bypass or eliminate the existing channels are threats to the very existence of the Washington system. The opposition of the Washington establishment to Jimmy Carter stems not from fundamental policy differences; it stems from a real fear that some exploiters might switch positions with some exploitees.

In the end, though, much of politics is exploitive. What else is new? I am most cynical about the operation of the Washington system for a second, more serious reason. Public policy emerges from the system almost as an afterthought. The shape of policy is a by-product of the way the system operates, rather than a consciously directed effort to deal with social and economic problems. Congressmen know that the specific impact of broad national policies on their districts is difficult to see, that effects are hidden, so to speak. They know too that individual congressmen are not held responsible for the collective outcome produced by 535 members of Congress. Thus, in order to attain reelection, congressmen focus on things that are both more recognizable in their impact and more credible indicators of the individual

congressman's power—federal projects and individual favors for constituents. In order to purchase a steady flow of the latter, congressmen trade away
less valuable currency—their views on public policy. The typical public law
is simply the outcome of enough individual bargains to build a majority.
Maybe that's just politics, but we don't have to like it, and political scientists
need not construct silly defenses for it.

The existence of the Washington system locks us into the New Deal way
of doing things: pass a law, appropriate a lot of money, and establish a new
federal bureaucracy. No reasoned analysis underlies that method of operation. The electoral interest of incumbent congressmen does. Critics used to
complain that we had a nineteenth-century Congress in a twentieth-century
world. Things have improved a bit: we now have a 1930s Congress in a 1970s
world. During the primaries in the spring of 1976 I listened with amusement
as the media echoed the congressional contenders' charges that Carter was
not specific on the issues. Never did the media stop to ponder whether the
congressional contenders might be specific but mindless. Prior to Carter's
move into the mainstream of the Democratic party, he was in fact the only
genuine hope for radical policy change. The congressional contenders were
the true conservatives despite their talk of federal activism. They had in mind
only one type of activism: centralized federal programs whose primary effect
would be to enrich the electoral coalitions that regularly return them to office.

The Washington system stifles genuine policy innovation. In recent years
we have heard talk about more flexible, less centralized policies involving
moves away from large federal bureaucracies. We should expect more talk
but little action in the near future despite Jimmy Carter's intentions. To lessen
federal control over the daily operation of the country is to lessen incumbent
congressmen's chances of reelection. So their voluntary cooperation is not
likely. Consider, for example, the revenue-sharing program, whose extension in 1976 encountered serious congressional difficulties. Representative
Barber Conable (R., New York) identified four sources of opposition. The
first includes those philosophically opposed to separation of the taxing and
spending powers. The other three facets of the opposition are, in Conable's
words:

> 2) A related group of power brokers, centered in our Appropriations
> Committee, who don't like any program over which they don't have
> direct and detailed control. Revenue sharing money doesn't have many
> federal strings tied on it, is automatically appropriated and automatical-

ly distributed, which makes it low priority money for those who want to throw their weight around in the distribution process.

3) Those congressional grumps who felt they didn't get much credit for the program, the benefits of which showed up in the local real estate tax rate and thus helped reelect local officials rather than congressmen.

4) Those grantsmen with political clout nationally, who because of their leverage with Congress and bureaucracy feel that they will do better than the average with selective categorical grants, and so don't want to see available community money watered down for them by automatic distribution to communities too weak to be good at grantsmanship.[1]

Even granting that Conable is a Republican and favorably disposed to revenue sharing, his analysis is plausible and suggests the difficulties likely to be faced by programs not cast from the traditional (that is, New Deal) mold. Professor Harold Seidman, a more disinterested observer, provides a similar, if more general, perspective:

> Decentralization makes an excellent theme for campaign speeches, but those who take campaign promises seriously run the risk of incurring congressional displeasure. Governors and mayors are competitors of Senators and Representatives. Once decisions are made outside of the Nation's capital, local officials can deal directly with Federal field staff and members of Congress are excluded from a key role in the decision-making processes. Constituents do not have to come to their congressman for assistance. What is worse, a local official may announce a Federal project or grant before the congressman can issue his press release.[2]

Even the reorganization of the federal bureaucracy in an attempt to improve efficiency generates little or no support among congressmen. When Richard Nixon proposed a large-scale cabinet reorganization and consolidation, the fate of the proposal could be read from the faces of the listening committee and subcommittee chairman. No chance. Democratic opposition to a Republican president? Not at all. I doubt that Jimmy Carter will fare any better. In the first flush of victory congressional leaders may voice support for reorganization in the abstract. Whether 250-odd House and Senate subcommittee chairmen will support a specific reorganization plan is a far different matter. Subgovernments built up over the years are potential victims of any federal reorganization, and few congressmen will sacrifice their smoothly operating subgovernment in order to help create a more smoothly operating government.

This, then, is the basis of the cynical view of the Washington system. The incentives of incumbent congressmen lead them to protect and encourage the structure and operation of a centralized bureaucratic state almost irrespective of the kind of public policy that constrains our present and shapes our future.

The Optimistic View

In district A I spoke to a Democratic state legislator who represents one of the most solidly Republican areas in the congressional district. "How do you do it?" I asked. He told me that although nominally a part-time politician, he spends seventy-eighty hours a week on political matters. During a biweekly radio spot he discusses legislative business and also announces his forthcoming schedule: A sample:

> On Monday night from 6:00 to 10:00 p.m. I will be at the fire station in Johnsburg. At the same Tuesday night I will be at the post office in Pearsville. At the same time Wednesday night I will be at the Elks in Dovertown, etc. Come on out and talk. Tell me what problems you have. Maybe I can help you.

He went on to argue that more people know him than know the congressman or senator, because car registrations and student loans touch people more directly than matters of national policy. While talking to me he thought he sensed disapproval or at least lack of admiration for his activities. He grew agitated.

> You've got to understand. The little guy just can't get through the bureaucracy. He can't get anything done. They ——— him over all the time. What a state representative can do is to protect the little guy and help the little guy. That's what you do to get reelected. That's the job of the elected official today.

The optimistic view of the Washington system generalizes the sentiments expressed by the state legislator. One can argue that in a complex post-industrial society big business, big labor, and big government must be accepted as givens. And given that the bureaucracy exists and will continue to exist, a critical need for ombudsman services exists and will continue to exist. So, instead of lamenting the decline of Congress as a policy-making body, we should rejoice in the vigor and effectiveness shown by contemporary congressmen in their ombudsman role. Somehow we have muddled through again as we have in the past. Our institutions have adapted themselves to the changing needs of the society.

Certainly the optimistic view contains an element of truth. Ombudsman services are needed, and congressmen do the job well. Congressmen, not surprisingly, are partial toward the optimistic view. One of Clapp's subjects observes:

> One reason we get the mail is because people either have not been able to find out with whom they should deal or have been exposed to a lot of red tape. The federal government is entering into the lives of people more and more, and the agencies are not known to them or are not near. Thus they think of their congressman. One of the most rewarding things we do is rectifying some of the erroneous decisions or lack of attention from administrative agencies to the problems of individual constituents. In many instances the executive branch is wrong, and the only recourse the individual has is to come to a senator or member of the House.[3]

Basically the optimistic view differs from the cynical view in two respects. First, it treats incumbent congressman as much more innocent than the cynical view. Incumbents are just public-spirited good ol' boys protecting their constituents from the ravages of the bureaucracy. Certainly they are not compounding the problem. Second, the optimistic view holds ombudsman activities in sufficiently high regard that it accepts the decline of the programmatic role of congressmen and Congress as a fair exchange or else considers that decline a reflection of an inevitable growth of executive dominance.

The optimistic view embodies an alternative explanation for the events and processes about which I have written. Perhaps it is the more correct explanation. If so, we could all sleep more easily.

The Alarmist View

I wish I could write that the alarmist view is merely the ultimate absurd extension of the cynical view. Unfortunately, not only do some reasonable (at least intelligent, if sometimes unreasonable) observers hold that view, but I can point to enough suggestive examples that I would hesitate to dismiss the alarmist view out of hand. The argument runs like this.

What began as harmless or even beneficial dabbling in bureaucratic affairs has become (or threatens to become) congressional addiction to the bureaucratic "fix." Each of the preceding two views presumes that congressmen have the upper hand in dealing with the bureaucracy. Do they? Will they always? As the federal role grows larger and larger, as more and more citizens are directly affected by bureaucratic decisions, will the bureaucracy come to dominate the Congress–bureaucracy relationship, at least on significant decisions? Will we reach a state in which the Congress becomes so dependent on the constituency service function that the bureaucracy has make-or-break power over congressmen or at least the ability to inflict great political pain and suffering?

Worrisome examples are easy to cite. When certain congressmen made noises about reducing the operating subsidies of Amtrak, the latter responded by unveiling plans for reduced operations. Just coincidentally, lines to be eliminated seemed to run through the districts of critical members of the Appropriations and Commerce committees. Just coincidence, of course, and no irrevocable decision had been reached. Amtrak just wanted Congress to know the lines along which it was thinking.[4]

Similarly, the congressman who threatens to rock the boat may find that a base, veterans' hospital, or important government program in his district is under consideration for possible elimination or termination. The story is an old one. When a school budget gets cut, the head bureaucrats announce that 2,000 classroom teachers must be released, or the football program will be eliminated. For some reason guidance counselors, deputy assistant principals, and other clerks are indispensable. Similarly, when city budgets are cut, firemen and on-the-beat policeman stand in danger of loss of employment. Apparently the city would shut down if any middling-level clerical jobs were eliminated. Bureaucrats are not without weapons in their struggles against elected officials, and the more the elected officials come to rely on favors from the bureaucrats, the more vulnerable they are to the cessation of those favors. He who lives by the boondoggle may die by it as well.

As one would expect, incumbent congressmen are aware of their growing vulnerability to bureaucratic decisions. Presumably they will search for ways to lessen that vulnerability. For example, during the defense appropriations debate of April 1976, House Majority Leader Tip O'Neill offered an amendment to prohibit the Department of Defense from reducing operations at any domestic military base by more than 50 percent unless Congress had been notified prior to March 15, 1973. This intriguing amendment would have given Congress a veto over the closing of any domestic military base (including 160 already targeted for closure or cutback by the Ford administration). The amendment failed, 152-202. During the debate Richard Ichord (D., Missouri) charged that "this amendment would require the operation of our defense forces not for the primary purpose of defending the United States, but for the economic concerns of local, self-serving interests." Apparently 152 congressmen approved of the latter point of view. On May 7, 1976, a weaker O'Neill amendment passed. This one provided that Congress should receive one year's notice prior to the closing or major cutback of any domestic military installation.[5]

In addition to such imaginative safeguards, congressmen can retaliate against uppity bureaucrats. The appropriations process is an annual event, and new program authorizations are constantly sought. But congressmen must stand for reelection every two years. A defeated congressman receives little solace from the knowledge that his buddies will avenge his defeat someday. Thus the better part of valor might simply involve no attempts to frustrate bureaucratic plans. Individual congressmen might find it much safer to accept the crumbs thrown to them by the bureaucracy and otherwise just not get in the way. They could continue to be congressmen, but real power would have passed to the hands of an appointive, self-perpetuating coterie of career officials.

The Three Views: Alternatives or a Developmental Sequence?

I do not consider the three viewpoints on the Washington system as mutually exclusive. Rather, I think they are views one might form by examining the system at three different points in time. In the early 1960s I suspect that most observers would have agreed upon the optimistic view. In the mid-seventies I believe that we are well into the cynical view. At some unspecified future time will the alarmist view constitute an accurate description rather than a discomforting scenario?

A Fourth View: Kill the Messenger

Before concluding this chapter I wish to mention a fourth viewpoint held by some doctrinaire liberals, particularly those doing well under the existing system. This viewpoint does not focus primarily on the Washington system itself; rather, it focuses on the motives of those who attack that system. Consider the following remarks (from a speech printed in the *Los Angeles Times*) by Vernon Jordan, executive director of the Urban League:

> In a few brief years our nation has moved from "we shall overcome" to "we don't care." That is the real meaning of the anti-Washington rhetoric we've been hearing in this presidential campaign. Cutting across the ideological spectrum and afflicting liberals and conservatives alike, it preaches a doctrine I call "The New Minimalism"—meaning less government, less spending, less federal manpower and less government regulation.
>
> Somehow, in their calculations, the New Minimalists don't include fat Pentagon budgets or tax expenditures that benefit the well-off. They ignore the fact that *less government means less protection for people without resources; that less spending means fewer desperately needed social programs and stark hunger for those in poverty; that fewer government employees means fewer public services; that less government regulation means an end to civil-rights enforcement* (my emphasis).[6]

Jordan's constituency has suffered horribly at the hands of white majority government in this country. Thus upon reading his attack any liberal Democrat feels a twinge of panic; there is an immediate temptation to search one's soul for a trace of racism or at least insensitivity to the plight of the have-nots in our society. Such temptations should be resisted, and Jordan's arguments should be recognized for what they are: nonsense.

To condemn the Washington system is not to say that we need less government or less humanistic government. It is simply to recognize that the present government has pathological aspects. What we do need is better government: more efficient, more flexible, and more creative government. If we had better government we could use existing levels of input to provide higher levels of services or lower levels of input to maintain existing levels of services. Naturally those interests faring well under the present system may hesitate to gamble on the chance of something better. But despite sympathy with their cause, we should not let them bully us into believing that we now live in the best of all possible worlds. All of this country's goodness, truth, and beauty does not dwell in the hearts of those who work in Washington, D.C.

Chapter 9
What Lies Ahead?

The Washington system grew up as the public sector expanded. At first the system was an unforeseen by-product of genuine attempts to legislate in the general interests of the American citizenry. Today the system has become an end in itself. It enables congressmen and bureaucrats to achieve their most dearly held goals by giving the appearance of satisfying the goals of the American people. In reality, public policy in this country is hostage to the personal goals of congressmen and the bureaucracy.

What lies ahead? Will the system continue to operate as presently or even degenerate into the bureaucratic state conjured up by alarmists (chapter 8)? Or can we expect or hope for more favorable developments? My personal viewpoint is pessimistic. I see little chance of any major changes in the operation of the Washington system, at least in the short term. The system is a response to people's incentives, and I do not see any potential sources of comparably strong incentives for change.

Congressmen, first of all, will not voluntarily acquiesce in the dismantling of the system. Congress embraces those reforms which advance the interests of its members and rejects most others. Even those congressmen who might win office by running against the system will find themselves subject to its temptations once they arrive in Washington.

Nor will the bureaucracy disrupt the operations of the system by ceasing to accommodate congressmen. To do so would invite great pain and suffering at the hands of frustrated congressmen. Besides the bureaucracy thrives under the system. Why on earth would it try to bring about change?

And the people? What is our incentive to change? Would we voluntarily give up our particular plums? Hardly. Each group in the population favors disconnecting the Washington system by elimination and reorganization of agencies and programs not related to its special preserve: "Let's you and him do away with the Washington system. My program is in the public interest."

Not only does each group in the population wish to maintain the status quo on matters relating to it, while changing it on matters relating to others, but, additionally, each group fights harder to preserve those programs from which it benefits than to eliminate or modify those programs from which it doesn't.[1] And given the way congressmen respond, the result is no change. We hear much talk about the seeming immortality of bureaucracies. Professor Herbert Kaufman, for example, recently published a short study on this topic.[2] He finds that of 175 organizational units existing in 1923—half a century ago— 148 of them still existed in 1973. And 246 new ones had grown up. But bureaucracies are not immortal; they are in fact weak. They achieve the appearance of immortality by building constituencies who scream to their congressmen when their agencies or their agencies' programs are endangered. *Bureaucracies are immortal only insofar as Congress grants them immortality.* And Congress bestows such grants only so long as congressmen can use the bureaucracies. And congressmen can use the bureaucracies only because we, the people, pay them in votes to use the bureaucracies. The enemy is us.

What of the currently popular "sunset laws?" These laws provide for automatic review of every agency or program after a specified interval of time. The laws carry a presumption of guilt: without positive action to extend the program or recharter the agency existence ceases. Does the current popularity of such laws (fifty-one cosponsors in the U.S. Senate) contradict what I have just written? Not really.

Those threatened by the elimination of an agency or program fight harder than those with a generalized interest in efficiency or costcutting. Thus the renewal process will be dominated by those with a material stake in preserving agencies and programs. Besides, consider the real import of the sunset laws: congressmen gain life and death power over every federal agency and program. In theory Congress has that power now, but it is a blunderbuss power, difficult to use. Ah, but when agencies and programs automatically die every five years, say, the use of that power becomes easier and the threat of it more credible. Rather than attempt positive action to eliminate a program, an unhappy congressman can quietly let it be known that he will not lift a finger to keep a program from dying. The sunset laws might prevent the present Washington system from degenerating into the bureaucratic state feared by the alarmists, but such laws will not upset the Washington system. To the contrary, *they will enhance the power of individual congressmen to extort constituency favors from the federal bureaucracy.* Even so, one should note that such proposals have received a more favorable reception in the Senate, a body more media-oriented, issue-oriented (and presidency-oriented) than the House. The representatives see little reason to tinker with a system that works very well for them already. In fact, members of the House were even somewhat leery of adopting President Ford's weak proposals for the reform of federal regulatory commissions and policies. The system works beautifully from their standpoint. Why tamper with a winner?

Although I am pessimistic, I am not absolutely so. Changes in the Washington system could arise from two different sources. But compared to the sturdy beams which hold up that system, these sources of change are fragile sticks. Probably they will not support our hopes.

First, the people could elect an outsider president committed to wholesale changes in the Washington system. (Perhaps they did so in 1976; as yet we cannot say.) If the issue became heated enough congressmen could be forced to acquiesce in modifications of the system. On the whole congressmen achieve reelection on the basis of constituency service, not issues. But that is not to deny that on occasion an issue becomes so important that congressional positions on that issue determine the vote. Civil rights, school busing, and abolition have been such issues, although never in the nation as a whole.

As I have argued, citizens will not voluntarily consent to give up those elements of the status quo from which they profit. But a majority might vote to coerce universal abandonment of federal boondoogles. The analogy is a familiar one. People do not voluntarily contribute an extra $100 to government, but they do vote for universally applicable tax raises. Individual incentives will not support piece-by-piece disconnection of the Washington system, but they might support wholesale dismantlement. The perception of universal sacrifice is critical.

In any case, the preceding argument is a frail one. At the least, conditions in the nation would need to grow much worse than they are to give the argument any real possibilities. And even so, when the bureaucratic fur hits the fan, we might all find that we'd rather live with the present system than experience the uncertainties inherent in changing our established ways.

The Washington system could change for a second, similarly weak reason. Quite simply, congressmen themselves might get tired of it. I mentioned in chapter 1 that the voluntary retirement rate of congressmen has risen during the early 1970s. A number of factors are probably at work. Congressional pensions have improved, for one thing. But additionally, some congressmen report that holding the office is just no fun anymore. Some refer to the poisoned atmosphere of Watergate-era Washington. Other responses give us some reason to hope. Speaker Carl L. Albert, for example, told the Associated Press that:

I think there is still a lot of personal satisfaction in serving in
Congress . . .

It's harder work than it used to be. There is a lot more work and there
is a lot more interruptions . . .

I spend a lot more hours than I used to on the chore type of work.[3]

Another retiree, James Hastings (R., New York), told the *Washington Post*
that one of his job frustrations was that his constituents didn't care about his
legislative accomplishments:

In the minds of many people those things don't count. Number one
they are not aware of them. And number two, what's important is what
I can do for them on a personal basis . . .

All a member of Congress needs to do to win reelection is run a good
public relations operation and answer his constituent mail promptly.

What kind of whore am I?[4]

Perhaps such sentiments will become widespread. Perhaps we've reached a
rough equilibrium between constituency service and public policy-making
within the congressional workload. Beyond a certain point congressmen
simply quit rather than shift any more effort from the latter to the former.

Recall that a former Republican congressman in district B implied that
many members of today's Congress could not earn $57,000 a year in the
private sector. Maybe he's right. But then again, as the tangible benefits of

the small society   by Brickman

HOO-BOY! THERE MUST BE MORE TO
LIFE THAN BEING REELECTED —

6-15
BRICKMAN

Distributed by Washington Star Syndicate

holding office increase, more capable individuals might seek the office. Such individuals might not be willing to spend their careers as errand boys. Moreover, confidence in their own capabilities could lead them to tolerate greater electoral risks than present incumbents. Defeat would not mean teaching school, selling insurance, or drawing up wills back in Possum Hollow.

I suspect there is too much optimism in the preceding paragraphs. But where else can we place our hopes? United States congressmen gave us the Washington establishment. Ultimately, only they can take it away.

PART TWO

Introduction to Part Two

The first edition of *Keystone* was an attempt to describe and evaluate some little-noted aspects of a transitional era in the history of Congress. What was changing and how is much clearer today than it was twelve years ago, though it is still far from transparent. In the first place, the 1970s was a period in which the committee-centered institution of the mid-century gave way to the more floor-centered institution of the 1980s. One subsection of chapter 7, "The Continued Decentralization of Congressional Power," describes the proliferation of subcommittees and speculates about the implications of that proliferation for congressional policy-making. This development, so striking in hindsight, has since received extensive treatment in the literature.[1] As I will discuss in chapter 12, the consequences of "subcommittee government" are still a matter of some debate; but at any rate, the internal operation of Congress today is strikingly different than it was in 1960.

Internal changes in Congress are only part of the transition, however. The flip side of the increased importance of constituency service in congressional elections is a decline in the importance of national forces. Studies in the past decade have documented the declining importance of presidential coattails and, with less certainty, the weakened impact of national economic conditions in congressional elections.[2] The House of Representatives, at least, is more insulated from national currents than in any previous period of American history.[3] The Senate requires a separate discussion.

Structural changes in the Congress and changes in the nature of congressional elections are not independent, however. In any democratic political system, electoral patterns, the structure of governmental institutions, and public policies will tend toward an equilibrium.[4] For example, where candidates win election largely on the basis of their own efforts, as in the contemporary United States, one expects a decentralized set of governing arrangements that produce unconnected, incoherent policies. Each element in the complex both reflects and supports the others. In contrast, where candidates win election on the basis of considerations that are almost completely beyond their control, such as national party affiliation in mid-century Britain, one expects more centralized governing arrangements that produce coherent policies, though such policies may reverse with each alternation of the governing parties. For convenience we often discuss internal and external aspects of Congress separately, but the two are inextricably connected.

Beyond changes in Congress, the 1970s was a period of transition in other aspects of our politics as well. The transformation of the presidential nomination process has changed the face of American politics.[5] The decline of party ties in the electorate, advances in communications and information technology, and an explosion in the number of interest groups and PACs have altered the conduct of campaigns. And finally, OPEC, stagflation, deficit politics, and Ronald Reagan have left their mark on national politics. These and other developments have led to corresponding modifications of what I thought in 1977.

Thus, the chapters in part 2 revisit the original text. The intervening years have seen a flood of research on congressional elections, so chapter 10 surveys some pertinent findings. Various arguments in *Keystone* have been misunderstood, so chapter 11 offers clarifications. The importance of several developments, such as the growth in PACs, has become apparent only in the intervening years, so chapter 12 discusses what now appear to be omissions and underemphases in the original text. A concluding chapter discusses the current state of national politics in light of all the preceding arguments and evidence.[6] All things considered—the passage of time, new evidence, captious criticism, and intervening developments—I am satisfied by how well the original argument has aged, and how little the essentials of the mature argument differ from those of the green version of twelve years ago.

Chapter 10
Some More-than-Circumstantial Evidence

This book began with a simple empirical finding: the average margins of House incumbents rose by 5–10 percent during the postwar period. In chapter 2 I discussed the potential significance of this shift in election outcomes. Depending on *why* member margins were increasing, larger margins could dampen the responsiveness of individual representatives to constituency sentiments, and the responsiveness of the collective Congress to changes in national sentiments. Chapter 3 examined several proposed explanations for the vanishing marginals, concluding that none of them was well supported by available evidence. Finally, chapters 4–6 developed another hypothesis— that government expansion had led to a change in popular perceptions of congressmen. Relative to the early postwar baseline, the electoral importance of constituency service had increased. Some circumstantial evidence consistent with this new hypothesis was presented in chapter 7.

As it turned out, the decade 1975–85 saw an outpouring of academic interest in congressional elections. *Keystone* was only an early entry in a line of books and articles that numbered in the hundreds.[1] Because this research has produced much information relevant to the arguments advanced in this book, I can now report evidence that is more than circumstantial. Most of this evidence is positive, but as would be expected, some of the new information is inconsistent with parts of my earlier arguments.

New Evidence: The Good

The most compelling pieces of circumstantial evidence contained in the first edition are the entries in table 5 of chapter 7. Between the 1950s and the 1970s personal staffs of members expanded, and their constituency presence surged.[2] These facts had previously been overlooked, but upon reflection they were not surprising. With the expansion in the scope and number of government programs in the postwar period, and considering the con-

---

Chapters 10–13 were drafted during the presidential campaigns of 1988.

gressman's traditional role as provider of constituency services, an expansion of service activity was only to be expected. But expected or not, the evidence in chapter 7 was only circumstantial because answers to other important questions were lacking. Had larger staff operations actually delivered a higher level of service? Perhaps staff were engaged more in advertising and public relations activities than in service. Even more important, did the apparent expansion of service activities actually produce the hypothesized changes? Did constituents increasingly view their representatives more in a nonpartisan, service frame, and less in a partisan, programmatic frame? After all, it was logically possible, if not likely, that the expansion in service activity went unnoticed by constituents.

Beyond these two fundamental questions were two other relevant questions. Did members believe that constituency service was electorally useful? The answer seems obvious, but again, it is logically possible that electoral advantage was an incidental by-product of service that went unnoticed by members. Though chapter 5 reproduced some pertinent quotations, more systematic evidence was unavailable. Finally, even if members believed that service was electorally advantageous, is that why they did it? Whatever the electoral effects, members' motives logically could be entirely divorced from electoral considerations.

We are now in a position to say something about each of the preceding four questions. To dispose of the simplest one first, the electoral payoffs of constituency service are widely acknowledged. During interviews with administrative assistants from 102 House offices in 1978, we asked whether constituency service enhanced members' electoral prospects. Only two asserted that service had no significant electoral effect.[3] Although some denied that hope of electoral reward was the primary rationale for service, belief in the reward was all but universal.

Tracing the perceptions of constituents across time turns out to be more difficult than one might expect. The surge in research on congressional elections has generated a wealth of data about constituent perceptions from 1978 onward, but the study of *change* requires data from earlier periods to provide a baseline. Only one detailed survey of congressional elections was conducted prior to 1978; that survey, executed in 1958, must bear nearly all the weight of temporal comparisons.[4]

Table 9 provides a plausible counterpart to table 5 of chapter 7. As the resources allocated to constituencies increased, reports of services rendered increased correspondingly. In the twenty years separating the two surveys,

Table 9. Percentage of Voters Seeking
Assistance, 1958 and 1978

Type of Casework	1958	1978
Help with problems	4.1%	10.8%
Information	1.5	9.8
Total	5.6	17.2

Source: 1958 and 1978 National Election Studies.

constituent requests for help and/or information approximately tripled. By 1978 more than a sixth of all reported voters claimed to have contacted their representatives for information or assistance.

Several pertinent features of casework requests should be noted. First, citizens generally are satisfied with the member's response: in recent years close to two-thirds of constituents report being "highly satisfied" and only one-eighth report being "dissatisfied." Thus, as argued in part 1, casework is almost always politically profitable; the probability of upside gain is much higher than that of downside loss. Second, those reporting casework requests also report higher levels of voting. And third, second-hand reports of casework done for friends and relatives are at least as numerous as personal requests, and satisfaction levels are similarly high.[5] In contemporary elections personal and second-hand casework alone are sufficiently important to account for a 5 percent edge in favor of the incumbent.[6]

Although a major component of constituency service, personal assistance to constituents is not the only form service takes. Aid in the procurement of particularized benefits (grants, contracts, projects) is a second major element. Both the 1958 and 1978 surveys asked constituents whether they could recall anything particular the member had done for the *district* as opposed to individuals. There was no increase across the twenty-year period in the *number* of affirmative responses—about one-third in each case. But as table 10 shows, the question elicited a hodgepodge of replies, and the only significant change in the pattern of comments is an increase in the fraction that refer specifically to local problems and projects.[7]

Thus, the increase in resources allocated to districts does correspond to constituent reports of higher levels of services. Does this correspondence show up in changes in congressional images? And if so, are these changed

Table 10. Nature of District Service Recalled by Constituents,
1958 and 1978

Substance of Recollection	1958	1978
General competence	8%	7%
Provides access to government	4	7
Communicates with constituents	7	4
National legislation, policy	22	22
Local problems/projects	30	42
Good party member	2	—
Group references	14	15
Negative comments	5	1
Other/miscellaneous	8	2

Source: 1958 and 1978 National Election Studies.

images reflected in changes in congressional voting? In both cases the answer
is yes.

In the election surveys constituents were asked to relate in their own words
the things they liked and disliked about their member of Congress. Table 11
compares the positive remarks made in 1958 and 1978.[8] Three changes in
popular perceptions are of special interest to this study. First and most important, the largest change in the pattern of comments occurs in the "attentiveness to constituency" category. The proportion of citizens making
positive comments in this category rose from one-tenth to one-quarter across
the twenty-year period bracketed by the surveys. This heightened tendency to
evaluate the representative in terms of constituency service goes hand in hand
with the increased allocation of resources to constituencies first documented
in chapter 7.

Table 11 shows two other changes that are not large enough to stand on
firm statistical ground but are highly suggestive nonetheless. First, the tendency to evaluate members of the House in partisan terms diminished almost
to the point of disappearing, consistent with an extensive literature on various
aspects of party decline.[9] Second, the tendency to evaluate representatives in
terms of issues and ideologies seems to have risen, counter to expectations
expressed in the first edition. I will have more to say about this finding below.

The changes in popular perceptions evident in table 11 carry over into
measurable changes in voting behavior. Statistical analyses of voting deci-

Table 11. Positive Evaluations of House Incumbents, 1958 and 1978

Category	1958	1978
General, good man	11%	7%
Experience and record	20	15
Personal attributes	30	30
Constituency attentiveness	11	25
Philosophy, ideology	2	7
Domestic issues/policy	3	5
Foreign policy	0+	1
Group references	6	5
Party affiliations/connections	5	1
Personal considerations	8	—
Other	4	4

Source: 1958 and 1978 National Election Studies.

sions in 1958 and 1978 indicate that each of the changes in the *substance* of perceptions reported in table 11 goes along with a corresponding change in the *importance* of those perceptions in House voting.[10] Constituency attentiveness comments were more common in 1978 than in 1958 *and* more important in determining how a citizen voted. Similarly, comments dealing with issues and ideologies were more common in 1978 *and* more important in determining how a citizen voted. Conversely, partisanship was a less frequent basis for evaluation in 1978 than in 1958 *and* a less important factor in determining how a citizen voted.

To sum up, in the aggregate an increased allocation of resources to the constituency goes along with (1) a higher incidence of constituent and district services reported, (2) an increased tendency to evaluate representatives in terms of constituency attentiveness, and (3) a greater impact of constituency service evaluations on House voting.

Of the four questions raised at the beginning of this section, one remains—that of motivation. Belief in the electoral yield of service is almost universal, but does the prospect of electoral gain motivate the constituency service activities of members? My colleagues and I have grappled with this question at some length elsewhere.[11] Motivation is a thorny issue. Individuals may not fully appreciate their own motives, and even when they do there is a natural human tendency to sugarcoat motivation, especially among politicians, a class of people whose stock-in-trade is the claim to higher motivation. In most cases the best evidence of motivation is indirect: does observed behavior comport with the assumed motive?

Such indirect evidence indicates that, at least to some degree, constituency service reflects electoral motives. If we examine changes in the size of personal staffs from one Congress to the next, it turns out that a consistently important predictor of staff size change is the member's previous election margin. The closer the previous election, the greater the size of the staff increase.[12] Similarly, the most junior representatives and others recently experiencing "close shaves" have the most aggressive constituency operations.[13] Thus, the picture that emerges is that, other things being equal, representatives who are "running scared" are the most energetic providers of constituency service—indirect evidence of electoral motivation to be sure, but probably as good as one can get.

New Evidence: The Bad

Some parts of the argument laid out in the original *Keystone* have not stood up so well as those just discussed, but happily this discussion of the bad calls is shorter than the discussion of the good ones. I use the term *bad call* in its everyday sense, an erroneous interpretation of something that has already happened, like calling a safe runner out. These are to be distinguished from speculations about future developments, some of which have not come to pass. The latter are discussed in chapter 12.

The errors of interpretation in the first edition turn out to be different aspects of a particular relationship: the relationship between legislative and service activity. In explaining table 11 above, I pointed out that the importance of issues and ideology to congressional voters appears to have increased somewhat. These are by no means dominant or even major factors in congressional voting. Only a small minority of the electorate recall how their representative voted on any particular bill, and only a bare majority offer an opinion about their members' general voting records.[14] Nevertheless, the importance of issue and ideological considerations appears to be somewhat greater today than it was twenty years ago, and I suspect it would be greater still were contemporary incumbents not so careful to avoid giving any ammunition to their opponents. This development runs counter to what I wrote in the first edition. At that time I suspected that the electoral importance of constituency service considerations had increased at the expense of legisla-

tive considerations. What appears to have happened instead is that the importance of both increased at the expense of partisanship and national tides set in
motion by administration performance. To adopt terminology that my colleagues and I have used elsewhere, the "personal vote" for members of
Congress has increased while the more impersonal vote, reflecting broader
forces such as partisanship and national conditions, has declined.[15]

This misreading of the importance of issue considerations in elections is
part of a larger misreading of the conflict between legislative and service
activities. The first edition waffled between what might be called a weak form
of the argument and a strong form. The weak form asserts that the expansion
of constituency service activity altered the image of the typical congressmen
in a positive way (see pp. 48–49). The strong form suggests that the expansion of service activity came at the expense of legislative activity (see pp. 57–
58). The strong form is apparently wrong.

In a review of the first edition, Norman Ornstein took exception to the
strong form of the argument.[16] If staffs and other resources had expanded
greatly, why was it not possible that both service and legislative activity—
indeed, all congressional activities—had increased? What reason was there
to think that the proportion of total congressional effort devoted to legislation
had declined, let alone the absolute amount? Ornstein saw no empirical basis
for such conclusions.

Subsequent research supports this criticism.[17] Casework, at least, is primarily a staff responsibility. Of course, members may become personally
involved when a case involves politically important constituents, and on
occasion a member's personal intervention can make the critical difference.
But the great bulk of the caseload is left to the staff.[18] Project work may
involve somewhat more personal effort by the members, especially insofar as
projects are explicitly written into legislation rather than awarded by the
agencies. But there is no indication that such concerns dominate the personal
schedules of many members.

While I concede error in viewing constituency service and legislative
work as competitive in the first edition, I am still not sanguine about the
changes that have occurred. First, although bountiful resources permit an
increase in the quantity of legislative work, the effect on the quality of work
remains in doubt. When *Keystone* was written, one still encountered the term
"Tuesday to Thursday club" in writings about Congress. This pejorative
term referred to East Coast congressmen who commuted home each week-
end, thereby shirking legislative responsibilities shouldered by their full-time

colleagues. One ceased to hear this term in the 1980s, because the entire Congress became a Tuesday-to-Thursday club. Important business normally is not scheduled on Mondays and Fridays because most members are somewhere in transit. Even if not engaged in the major components of constituency service—case and project work—members are deeply involved in the larger complex of activities that demonstrate constituency attentiveness. With three- or four-day Washington work weeks, it is not clear that members spend more of their personal time on legislative matters today than they did a generation ago. As Davidson and Oleszek observe (from their vantage point in the Congressional Research Service):

> It is at least arguable that ever more demanding electoral and ombuds-
> man functions have helped erode the legislative and institutional
> folkways identified by observers in the 1950s and early 1960s—
> especially the folkways of specialization, apprenticeship, and institu-
> tional loyalty. At the very least, it has placed added demands on
> members' time and energies. Although most ombudsman activities are
> actually carried out by staff aides rather than by members themselves,
> there are inescapable costs to members' schedules. Larger staffs, while
> helping lawmakers extend their reach of involvement, require supervi-
> sion and have a way of generating needs of their own. And with high
> constituent expectations, there are inescapably many symbolic func-
> tions that cannot be delegated to staffs—situations that require
> members' personal intervention and face-to-face presence. [19]

As Davidson and Oleszek note, an expert, full-time legislative staff can relieve members of much of the load. But second-hand research and study have their price. Moreover, thoughtful observers worry about the decline of deliberation in Congress, about the displacement of member-to-member negotiation by staff-to-staff negotiation, and in general about the influence now accorded to congressional staffs. [20] These matters will be taken up in chapter 12.

There is yet another reason why an apparent upsurge in the importance of legislative activities should not be taken at face value. Mayhew cautions us to distinguish position taking from legislative accomplishment. [21] Position taking involves being on the right side, saying the right thing, demonstrating the right sentiments. On major issues congressmen cannot be credited with or held responsible for legislative outcomes, because these are determined by the full membership of both chambers and the president. But the member fully controls his or her personal positions. Thus, members have strong electoral incentives to take carefully considered positions, but much weaker incentives to worry about legislative follow-up or future program results. With weak party constraints, capable staff, and access to the newest technology, members easily can construct detailed issue profiles that maximize appeal to their constituencies, but this activity has two potential costs. First, when each member considers it both proper and electorally important to kibitz every issue, it is more difficult to construct coalitions in support of a collective (party or presidential) program. Second, if voters respond to carefully designed and packaged positions, but pay less attention to broader outcomes, they encourage a government of posturing rather than one of performance.

In sum, constituency service apparently has not grown in importance at the expense of legislative work. Both have grown in importance at the expense of broader considerations such as party. But higher levels of legislative work made possible by resource expansion do not necessarily produce an improved legislative product. They may, but the jury is still out.

Whatever their nature, the enhanced importance of legislative considerations in House elections leads to a third correction in my original argument. In chapter 2 I noted that, depending on the reasons for the rising margins of incumbents, the responsiveness of individual members to their constituencies might diminish. After concluding that constituency service produced the larger margins, I felt that responsiveness was indeed a concern. But if issues and ideology are at least as important in congressional voting today as they were a generation ago, there is no reason to believe that responsiveness to districts has declined.[22] And undoubtedly it hasn't. In *Unsafe at Any Margin*, Thomas Mann argued that contemporary congressmen were psychologically insecure whatever the objective indications of electoral security.[23] Similarly, Gary Jacobson has argued that contemporary congressmen "run scared," and that by every indirect indicator, today's incumbents are as responsive as those of earlier eras.[24] I agree with these observations. The increased importance of constituency service has not come at the expense of policy responsiveness. Rather, both waxed in importance as partisanship and national forces waned.

This development does not alleviate all concerns about electoral responsiveness, however. Chapter 2 did not express a concern only or even primarily for *district* responsiveness. Rather, it pointed out that rising margins might insulate congressmen from *national* forces that historically produced the majorities enabling presidents to chart a new course. This has indeed come to pass. The House of Representatives has become a Democratic fiefdom as Republicans have been unable to translate vote gains into seat gains as successfully as in past eras. This is a topic to which I will return in the final chapter.

New Evidence: The Ugly

The first section of this chapter recounted a chain of evidence running from expanded service activity to reports of higher service levels to changes in popular perceptions of congressmen to changes in voting behavior. This chain supports the weak form of the argument that I offered in the first edition, but some scholars want more—a "smoking gun." Aggregate patterns are not enough, in their view. Rather, they attempt to show that those congressmen who are most heavily engaged in constituency service have electoral margins that directly correspond to service levels. As it turns out, service and resource levels do correlate with reputations, and reputations are strongly related to the vote, but scholars have failed to find a clear, direct link between constituency service in each district and the corresponding electoral outcome.[25] Apparently, there is a critical gap between argument and evidence.

Let us first place this criticism in context by noting all the factors researchers have failed to link to electoral margins. One or more studies have concluded that *each of the following has no direct link to electoral results:*

1. Casework
2. Federal spending in the district
3. Travel to the district
4. Size of staff (district or total)
5. Campaign spending
6. Campaign communications
7. Legislative activity (bills sponsored, committees served on)

Moreover, none of these factors has been linked to the ability to raise campaign funds or to the strength of the challenge faced by incumbents.[26] The literal implication of this collection of findings is quite ugly. The latest academic research appears to show that members of Congress can close up their district offices, dismiss their staffs, spend weekends in Washington with their families, quit doing casework, abandon the quest for federal funds, discontinue their newsletters, tell fat cats and PACs to buzz off, and *nothing will happen to them.*

For the most part political scientists are honorable people with no particular desire to mislead politicians, let alone one another. But collectively we certainly have sown confusion about the relationship between political resources and electoral outcomes. Various methodological and logical problems underlie this curious collection of findings. These have been elaborated elsewhere, but I will mention two of them more briefly here.[27]

First, the available data (on staff, offices, caseloads, and so forth) only imperfectly measure the pertinent variables—the quantity and quality of constituency service. One office's staff may be smaller but more efficient than another's. One congressman may have the district offices handle the caseload, while another centralizes the operation in Washington. The fact that Representative X has three district offices while Representative Y has only one may signify not that X performs three times as much service as Y, but only that X's district has three times as much land area as Y's. We can try to take account of many such variations, but it is impossible to take account of all of them, and do it simultaneously. When making gross comparisons of averages taken twenty years apart, the crudeness of the data does not prevent the patterns from emerging. But when seeking fine distinctions among individuals within a single election year, the noise in the data swamps the underlying pattern.

The second explanation for the general failure to find direct links between members' activities and their electoral margins is more subtle. It involves what statisticians call a "simultaneity problem," and it plagues research in this area. The most graphic illustration has come from research on campaign spending. Gary Jacobson reported that "the more incumbents spend, the worse they do."[28] What he found was not that campaign spending was harmful to incumbents, other things being equal. Rather, he found that other things were typically not equal in that incumbents who raised and spent the most did so because they were in trouble—they faced strong challenges that were destined to cut their margins, if not worse.

An equally striking example comes from an examination of district offices and incumbent reputations. As shown in table 12, the more district offices members had in 1978, the *lower* the proportion of their constituents who believed they would be helpful if the occasion arose. Could the establishment

Table 12. Typical Simultaneity Problem

# of District Offices	Incumbent Would Be Very Helpful (% of Total)
1	35
2	27
3	20
4	15
5	9

Source: 1958 and 1978 National Election Studies.

of district offices really be politically damaging? Of course not. A closer look at the data reveals that members with many district offices had constituents who did not know them very well—one-third had no idea at all of whether the representative would be helpful. Such representatives on average were more junior and more electorally insecure. Thus, district offices do not cause fuzzy reputations and electoral insecurity; just the opposite—fuzzy reputations and electoral insecurity are part of the reason members set up more district offices.

Here is an example of a simultaneity problem in schematic form:

	t_1	Service	t_2
Representative S	63%	Average	66%
Representative M	51%	High	62%

At time t_1 Representative S (safe) wins by a very comfortable 63 percent. She allocates an average level of resources to constituency service, performs reasonably well in other ways, and is reelected at time t_2 by a slightly larger margin. Representative M (marginal), in contrast, squeaks by at time t_1 by a narrow 51 percent. He responds with maximum levels of service, and at t_2 achieves reelection by a much larger 62 percent. His activities paid off handsomely. But note that a look at comparative electoral performance at time t_2 would find that the member who did more service did more poorly than the one who did less. The problem is that the positive effect of service is more than counter-balanced by the disadvantage in initial conditions.

This example appears to suggest that a before-and-after research design is the answer to the problem. That would be an improvement, but problems still remain, as illustrated by the following slightly more complex example:

	t_1	Service	Challenge	t_2
Representative S	63%	Average	Token	66%
Representative M	51%	High	Serious	53%

Because Representative S wins by such a comfortable margin at time t_1, she attracts only token opposition at time t_2. But because M wins by such a small margin at time t_1, he gets targeted by the other party's national committee and attracts a strong, well-funded challenger. After a tough campaign, he pulls through with a slightly improved margin. What will research show? The before-after comparison finds that the member who did more service showed a smaller improvement than the one who did less. But what the comparison doesn't show is that without his intensive service effort, Representative M might have been defeated.

In theory one can dissect and analyze problems like these, but in practice they are exceedingly difficult owing to data availability and the seemingly insurmountable requirements of the statistical techniques.[29] The bottom line is that the smoking gun will never be found (unless congressmen let us run controlled experiments with their offices and careers). At the national level we can show that service levels have increased, and that constituent perceptions and electoral margins have followed. But attempts to study district-by-district variation within particular Congresses are as likely to confuse as to illuminate.

Chapter 11
Confusions and Clarifications

In public, authors graciously take responsibility for the misunderstandings of readers. In private, they complain about careless reading or even malicious misreading. Over the years I have encountered a number of common misunderstandings of the arguments in *Keystone*. Some of these are primarily the fault of the reader, while others are primarily my fault.

Clarification 1: Constituency Service Is Not the Only Factor in Congressional Elections

On several occasions critics have offered examples of elections they believe were determined by presidential coattails, money, issues, a TV commercial, or some other factor than constituency service. Certainly, that is so: many factors affect the voting in House elections. *Keystone* never suggested otherwise. As explained in chapter 1, the average margins of House incumbents rose about 5 percent—from 60 to 65 percent—between the 1950s and the 1970s.[1] I argued that the expansion of constituency service was a likely explanation for that rise, *not* for the entire 65 percent of the vote garnered by the average incumbent. Moreover, chapter 5 reiterated that the actual electoral change we were seeking to explain was "marginal"—about 5 percent, clearly less than 10 percent.

Constituency service is *not* the sole or even the most important factor in House elections. For one thing, party identification still determines more votes than any other single factor.[2] If I were a member of Congress I would surely rather have a district with a 70-30 registration edge for my party than any number of offices and staff.

Nothing just said, however, denigrates the electoral importance of constituency service. Two points should be kept in mind. First, politicians understandably pay disproportionate attention to smaller electoral factors that are under their control—such as constituency service—than to larger electoral factors that are beyond their control—such as the partisan composition of their districts.[3] Second, small electoral differences and changes can have large political consequences. In particular, important things happen in the neighborhood of 50 percent. As margins rise above 50 percent, incumbents become less likely to be swept from office by an electoral triumph for the other party's presidential candidate. When margins rise, incumbents may look that much more formidable to potential primary and general election challengers, some fraction of whom are discouraged from making the race.

In sum, constituency service grew in electoral importance between the 1950s and 1970s, while party and other factors declined. Whether the relative importance of constituency service vis-à-vis other factors increased from, say, 10 to 20 percent of the explanation of the vote, or from 40 to 50 percent, is not a question I addressed. And given the lack of suitable data for the period before the increase, it remains a question without a precise answer.

Clarification 2: Constituency Service Is Not the Only Explanation of the House Incumbency Advantage

The misconception underlying this second clarification is similar to that underlying the first, though I am more to blame here. When *Keystone* was written, the advantage of incumbency was believed to be in the range of 5–8 percent. I considered several explanations—advertising, behavioral change by voters, redistricting—and concluded that the evidence failed to support them. Increases in constituency service activities were offered as an alternative explanation. I did not claim that service was the only possible explanation, just that it was the only one still in the race.

While I still believe that increased constituency service can easily account for increases of 5–8 percent in incumbents' margins, additional research has suggested other possible explanations for incumbent strength. Before discussing these, let us note that although redistricting arguments continue to have some adherents, especially among Republicans, careful academic studies continue to find no systematic advantage to incumbents from redistricting.[4] Similarly, there is still no solid evidence that incumbent strength reflects sheer name recognition produced by advertising. Incumbent congressmen are no better known today than they were a generation ago.[5] If it leaves a mark at all, advertising probably does so on the *substance* of voter perceptions.[6]

Three additional sources of incumbent strength have been suggested. First, modern information and communication technology have enhanced the capacity of politicians to track the sentiments of constituents and target specific audiences with suitable messages. While strong parties might constrain the ability of their members to adopt this "every man for himself" strategy, today's parties are less of a constraint than they were even a generation ago. True, the available evidence indicates that only a small minority of constituents have any information on the issue stands of their representatives, but the size of that minority is larger than it was a generation ago, and the influence of issues on its vote is clear.[7] Thus, carefully tailored issue stances probably contribute in some measure to the strength of contemporary incumbents.

A second seemingly obvious source of incumbent strength is money. Congressional races have gotten much more expensive over time, and the gap between incumbent and challenger finances has widened.[8] I will discuss PACs in a later chapter, but two points should be made here. First, the absolute level of challenger spending appears to be more important than the relative differential. Because all incumbents begin with an impressive level of taxpayer-provided resources (staffs, offices, communications technology, and so forth), campaign money appears to have lower marginal benefit for them than for challengers. Indeed, very high levels of incumbent spending can indicate weakness rather than strength: the incumbent goes all out to meet a serious challenge.[9]

Second, whatever the importance of campaign funding today, PACs and the explosion in campaign expenditures are a mid- to late-1970s phenomenon. The changes in congressional elections discussed in *Keystone* were concentrated in the mid- to late 1960s. So, while any discussion of incumbent strength in contemporary elections must deal with money, the importance of money for the arguments I advanced twelve years ago is probably lower.

A third explanation for the advantage of incumbency is different from most of the others in not focusing on incumbents. According to this explanation, challenger weakness not incumbent strength, is the key. The genesis of this explanation lies in late-1970s research that revealed how poorly challengers were known by constituents, how little money they spent, and how few of them displayed any apparent qualifications for office.[10]

One immediate observation is that challenger weakness at a single point in time—the 1970s—does not explain the *rise* in the advantage of incumbency. Incumbents on average have handily dispatched their opponents throughout the twentieth century. Thus, to support the challenger weakness argument one must show at the least that challenger quality declined *over the same period that incumbent margins increased*. The little data that exists does not

support this suggestion.[11] There is a plausible argument why strong challenges may have declined in frequency, though proponents of the challenger
weakness argument have not made it. As party organizations declined relative to individual candidate organizations, challengers were left without a
natural base of support and resources—the base formerly provided by party
organizations. While incumbents were similarly deprived, they were able to
vote themselves office, staff, and communications resources to replace whatever they lost from party sources. This argument will be developed at length
in chapter 12.

A second observation concerns the logical status of the challenger weakness explanation. To some extent challenger strength is endogenous, to use a
technical term. What it means is that the strength of challengers is in part
determined by the strength of incumbents. An incumbent with a history of
comfortable margins, an overflowing war chest, and a reputation for invin-
cibility scares away ambitious prosecutors and state legislators who are natural antagonists. (The image is that of wolves cowering before a grizzly.) In
contrast, the incumbent with declining margins, a shortage of funds, and a
reputation for ineptitude attracts strong challengers. (The image is that of
sharks circling a thrashing presence in the water.) While attempts to verify
this argument empirically have been inconclusive, every observer of electoral politics will attest to the prevalence of such beliefs.[12]

Clarification 3: Human Beings Are Not All Ivan Boeskys (but not Mother Teresas either)

Any argument in the social sciences reflects a particular worldview—a set
of basic assumptions about the structuring of social reality. For example,
Marxists attach primacy to the relationship of collective actors called classes
to the means of production. Pluralism, in contrast, emphasizes the competition of groups organized at a much finer level than social classes. The arguments developed in *Keystone* are set within the "rational-choice" approach
to political science. This approach views individuals as the fundamental
actors in politics and seeks to explain political processes and outcomes as
consequences of their purposive behavior. Political actors are assumed to
have goals and to pursue those goals sensibly and efficiently.[13]

To generate substantive propositions from rational-choice arguments, one
must specify the goals held by particular actors—simply to say that people
pursue their goals does not lead very far. In principle, any goal is permissible.

As Anthony Downs wrote thirty years ago, "It is possible for a citizen to receive utility from events that are only remotely connected to his own material income. . . . Some citizens would regard their utility incomes as raised if the government increased taxes on them in order to distribute free food to starving Chinese."[14] The example is dated, but not the point. The goal of a religious figure might be to maximize the number of souls saved, or to maximize total contributions to his ministry; the goal of a medical researcher to save lives, or to maximize the probability of a Nobel Prize; the goal of a senator to protect the security of Israel, or to maximize campaign contributions. In principle, rational-choice analyses can proceed with any specification of goals whatsoever.

In practice, two features of rational-choice analyses tend to arouse the ire of critics. The less important of these is the assumption of common motivation: analyses often posit that all actors of a particular type have the same goal. Thus, the clergy are maximizing souls saved, firms are maximizing profits, and bureaucrats are maximizing budgets. Researchers who make such assumptions realize of course that individual variation exists, but models grow too complicated to be useful if they try to reproduce the complexity of social reality.[15] Thus, one selects the most prevalent motivation among the actors one studies and works with that one alone. Arguments will be more convincing and more empirically accurate to the extent that the motivational assumption is accurate.[16]

The second, more inflammatory feature of rational-choice arguments is the tendency of practitioners to assume goals best described as "self-interested." For some reason the thought processes of otherwise intelligent persons short-circuit upon encountering this term. They make a sudden leap to images of Scrooge, Teapot Dome, the Teamsters, Michael Deaver—even Marcos and Noriega. They conjure up visions of the most venal, short-sighted pursuit of material gain. "Not all people are like that," they shout with outrage. True, not all people are.

The term *self-interest* as used in rational-choice analyses has much more limited connotations.[17] It simply means that individuals pursue their own goals, whether base or admirable, rather than the goals of others. It is true that on a scale ranging from base to laudable, rational-choice goal assumptions tend to lie closer to the former than to the latter, but that simply reflects the subsidiary assumption that individuals have goals appropriate to the institutional positions around which their careers are centered.

Congressmen are assumed to have a predominant reelection motive. In fact, 90 percent of them seek reelection every two years, most of them expending great amounts of effort and resources in pursuit of that end. No close observer of Congress can doubt that members are highly attuned to the electoral consequences of their actions. True, not every decision they make has electoral consequences; on such electorally insignificant decisions they are free to seek other ends, including the public interest.[18] On occasion a member will even take an electoral gamble because some other goal is sufficiently valued. President John F. Kennedy put his name on a book recounting a number of such examples. But if they were frequent, let alone the norm, there would have been no reason to write the book at all, let alone reason to entitle it *Profiles in Courage.*[19]

Bureaucrats are assumed to have a predominant interest in expanding their agencies' responsibilities and budgets. Is this so unreasonable or implausible? How many bureaucrats recommend cuts in their previous year's budget? How many recommend the abolition of programs under their jurisdiction? Derthick and Quirk note with satisfaction the Civil Aeronautics Board's development of a plan for its own abolition.[20] Why is the example so striking? Because it is so abnormal.[21]

Moving beyond those whose livelihood comes from the public sector, voters are usually assumed to have goals appropriate to their occupational, geographic, and social positions.[22] Of course, most citizens have a vision of politics that extends beyond their own pecuniary interests, but how many professors lobby their representatives to cut the research budget of the National Science Foundation? How many students advocate the abolition of student loan subsidies? How many blacks oppose affirmative action? How many tobacco farmers urge Jesse Helms to abandon his support of tobacco price subsidies? How many trial lawyers favor no-fault auto insurance? How many defense contractors oppose SDI? One could go on indefinitely. Naturally, group representatives can and do defend their positions in terms of justice and the public interest. But does anyone really doubt the motive force of private interest in determining many of the positions people hold?[23]

To some degree the preceding question need not even arise, for in many instances all analysis requires is agreement on intermediate goals rather than ultimate ends. For example, on pages 39–40 of the first edition of *Keystone* I wrote:

Even those congressmen genuinely concerned with good public policy must achieve reelection in order to continue their work. Whether narrowly self-serving or more publicly oriented, the individual congressmen finds reelection to be at least a necessary condition for the achievement of his goals.

And similarly on page 40:

As with congressmen, the specified goals apply even to those bureaucrats who genuinely believe in their agency's mission. If they believe in the efficacy of their programs, they naturally wish to expand them and add new ones. All of this requires more money and more people. The genuinely committed bureaucrat is just as likely to seek to expand his agency as the proverbial empire-builder.

As these passages indicate, despite vastly different ultimate goals, the same conclusions follow if satisfaction of an intermediate goal, such as reelection or budget expansion, is a precondition for achieving the ultimate goal. Imagine a member of Congress devoted above all else to ending apartheid in South Africa. If this member believed that no competitor could be more effective in bringing about that outcome, she would play the electoral game just as intensely—perhaps more so—than a member who was only interested in holding office for the status and prestige it conferred.

Discussions like these cannot achieve closure because the motives of political actors are not susceptible to direct investigation. In the first place, individuals may not be fully aware of their own motivations, and in the second place, they are likely to put the most favorable construction on their actions.[24] The investigative strategy adopted by scholars of the rational-choice school is to make plausible assumptions about motivation, then compare the logical implications with the patterns we observe in the world. Critics are welcome to make high-minded assumptions about human motivations. I will continue to make somewhat unflattering assumptions about motivations. I am betting that in the long run the latter approach will have more to say about American politics than the former.[25]

Clarification 4: This Book Is Not Immoral

The preceding clarification focused on the empirical accuracy of self-interest assumptions in rational choice arguments. Some critics, like Steven Kelman, worry that regardless of the analytic usefulness or empirical accuracy of rational-choice arguments (which they doubt), such arguments are immoral because they have corrosive effects on democratic politics. They weaken a useful mythology about the nobility of public service, and in fact serve to legitimize its opposite—the use of government to serve one's private interests.[26] Here Kelman commits the common professorial fallacy of vastly overestimating his impact on the world, but even if he were correct in assessing the importance of professors' scribblings, I would reject his critique. Moreover, I do so without recourse to the standard academic argument that the proper function of research scholars is to advance the state of knowledge and let the chips fall where they may. That is a legitimate argument that I accept under most circumstances, but Kelman evidently is speaking as a man of affairs rather than as a scholar, so his indictment requires a response of a more practical character.

The self-interest assumptions that underlie the analysis in *Keystone* are much the same assumptions that underlie the architecture of the American political system. Readers of the *Federalist* will recall the frequent unflattering references to human character: "infirmities" and "depravities" (Madison, no. 37), "despicable frailty" and "detestable vices" (Hamilton, no. 70), and "ordinary depravity" (Hamilton, no. 78). Wright observes that "the most striking and most important element in the theory of human nature expressed in *The Federalist* is that men are not to be trusted with power because they are selfish, passionate, full of whims, caprices, and prejudices."[27] Depravities, passions, and caprices can reasonably be interpreted as eighteenth-century synonyms for what we now know as self-interest.[28]

As for what was the exception and what the norm, Madison (no. 37) remarks:

> The history of almost all the great councils and consultations held among mankind . . . is a history of factions, contentions and disappointments, and may be classed among the most dark and degraded pictures which display the infirmities and depravities of the human character. If, in a few scattered instances, a brighter aspect is presented, they serve only as exceptions to admonish us of the general truth; and by their lustre to darken the bloom of the adverse prospect to which they are contrasted.[29]

Now, did the framers repress their personal experience and ignore the lessons of history so as not to weaken useful mythologies, as Kelman would recommend? Of course not. The framers reasoned that institutions must be designed so as to make use of or at least dissipate the harmful effects of self-interest: "Ambition must be made to counteract ambition. The interests of the man must be connected with the constitutional rights of the place" (Madison, no. 51).

As the Founders saw it, institutional designers should plan for the worst and hope for better. To do otherwise was dangerous. Certainly, human beings have a virtuous as well as a "depraved" side.[30] But if institutions are based on pessimistic expectations and officeholders prove more virtuous than expected, no great harm is done; whereas if institutions are premised on optimistic expectations, and officeholders fall short, the costs will be high. As for the utility of popular beliefs that public officials are motivated by a sincere search for the public interest, Hamilton's comment (no. 25) suggests that the framers would not have shared Kelman's enthusiasm for such useful mythologies:

> For it is a truth, which the experience of ages has attested, that the people are always most in danger when the means of injuring their rights are in the possession of those of whom they entertain the least suspicion.

Not only is the American system founded on the axiom that most people most of the time will act according to their own self-interest, but until quite recently the most noteworthy observers of American politics have viewed its actual functioning in that light. Though he found much that he admired in America, the premier antebellum commentator, Alexis de Tocqueville, had few illusions about American politics. For example, he wrote:

> It is impossible to consider the ordinary course of affairs in the United States without perceiving that the desire to be reelected is the chief aim of the President; that the whole policy of his administration and even his most indifferent measures, tend to this object; and that, especially as the crisis approaches, his personal interest takes the place of his interest in the public good.[31]

Similarly, the great late-century observer Lord Bryce did not see the public interest as the animating force in American (or any other country's) politics: "To rely on public duty as the main motive power in politics is to assume a comonwealth of angels. Men such as we know them must have some other inducement."[32] The early pluralists (ill-advisedly) banished the concept of public interest altogether, seeing politics as no more than a ceaseless struggle among interest groups.[33] In fact, academic political science did not take a Pollyannaish turn until the past generation or so.[34] Had *Keystone* been written anytime prior to 1940 it would certainly not have been criticized on moral grounds. Viewed from a historical perspective, this book is as American as apple pie.

Clarification 5: Congress Sometimes Adopts "Good" Policies

This clarification follows on the previous one, though the misconception it addresses rises from the incompleteness of my earlier discussion. Some critics seem to believe that the adoption of any policy that is deemed "good" by nonpartisan experts contradicts the arguments offered in this book. Deregulation of the airlines, the Social Security rescue of 1983, and the 1986 tax revisions are commonly cited as "counterexamples" to arguments that self-interest is the wellspring of politics.

Although some proponents of self-interest arguments have gone to considerable lengths to find narrow self-interest lurking beneath public policies like those cited, I do not find specific examples of "good" public policy at all puzzling, let alone troubling for my arguments. The misconception here is a special case of a more general one: the equation of motives and outcomes. Naïve observers sometimes assume that good motives produce good policies, and conversely (and in opposition to the Founders), that good policies reflect good motives. Of course, neither supposition is correct.

Popular wisdom recognizes the insufficiency of good motives: "The road to hell is paved with good intentions." And the political world abounds with examples of well-intentioned policies and programs that produced results ranging from disappointing to disastrous. Clearly, noble motives can produce rotten outcomes. But even if one concedes that good intentions are not sufficient, some disagree with the Founders and maintain that good intentions are at least necessary. How can good policy result from less-than-good intentions? In fact, there are a number of ways that ordinary, self-interested motives can produce good outcomes. This country could not have survived so long if that were not so.

This book emphasizes the geographic connection between representatives and constituents. Because each member is elected by people who inhabit a particular piece of territory, representatives are naturally more solicitous of the interests of that piece of territory than of the interests of other pieces of territory. Moreover, no one member can plausibly claim credit for advancing the interests of the nation as a whole (peace, low inflation, reducing the trade deficit, and so forth). Thus, the political incentives are to pursue local interests and discount adverse national effects.[35] Members who represent auto-producing districts attempt to restrict imports even if the costs to consumers and exporters far exceed the benefits to autoworkers. Representatives of farm districts advocate subsidy programs even if the national costs outstrip the local gains. Representatives of energy-producing districts seek advantages for producers even if those advantages pale before the national damages. As political scientists have repeatedly observed, congressmen understand the national interest only when it speaks in a local dialect.

The strong local orientation created by political ambition within a single-member district system generates a "distributive tendency" in congressional policy-making.[36] Members of Congress regularly formulate and revise programs so as to create opportunities to benefit their districts. The cost of such activity can be the destruction of program coherence and the dissipation of program resources. Model Cities, the Economic Development Administration, and much of military procurement are well-known examples.[37] To make matters worse, modern technology reinforces distributional considerations by enabling congressmen to sit in committee rooms with Lotus spreadsheets detailing the financial impact of various proposals on their districts.

Despite the strength and prevalence of the distributive tendency, there are circumstances under which it can be contained. In chapter 8 I discussed revenue sharing, a program that automatically distributed federal funds to localities but provided minimal opportunities for congressmen to claim credit. This program was widely supported by policy analysts, especially when compared to the categorical grants it was designed to replace, but because of its lack of political benefits it was never popular with congressmen. Nevertheless, the program was passed and several times renewed. Why? In large part because local officials and their organizations strongly supported such no-strings-attached funds.[38] Congressmen who sought to maintain good relations with important people in their districts had to restrain their normal inclinations and support a program that had little appeal for many of them.[39]

Thus, one constraint on congressional particularization of public policy is the existence of influential interest groups sophisticated enough to look beyond the simple adoption of programs and make demands about the shape programs take as well. If such groups foresee that unchecked congressional politics will vitiate the aims of their proposals, they can demand that congressmen support some features of programs and reject others. A large, well-endowed, nationally-organized group can persuade a majority of Congress to act counter to their normal tendencies. Somewhat ironically, then, "powerful special interests" may pressure government to serve their constituencies, but given that they will be served, organized interests may push Congress toward greater programmatic efficiency.

Interests organized on some basis other than geography provide another constraint on the distributive tendency. For example, Representative (formerly professor) David Price (D., North Carolina) has pointed out that the late Senator Warren Magnuson (D., Washington) discovered his latent dedication to consumerism after a close call in the 1962 Washington election. His staff decided that changing home-state political conditions made being the senator from Boeing an insufficient guarantee of reelection.[40] By cultivating an interest not organized on a geographic basis, Magnuson was able to change his image in a way that profited him politically. Similarly, Senator Edward Kennedy (D., Massachusetts) was persuaded by free-market arguments in the case of airline deregulation. Coincidentally, the issue was politically attractive for a tax-and-spend Democrat in an era of limits, especially for one with presidential aspirations.

So, what appears to be universalistic, far-sighted public policy may instead reflect the efforts of political actors other than congressmen who take a more sophisticated view of their interests and induce Congress to act accordingly. Local interests come first for congressmen; they vote. But more broadly organized interests possess resources as well, so political calculations will sometimes dictate that they have their way. Environmentalists, consumers, and senior citizens are contemporary examples. These nongeographic, group-centered influences on Congress were not sufficiently recognized in the first edition of this book.[41] Of course, nothing guarantees that interest groups will seek policies that serve broader interests, though I think that the broader the group, the more likely that will be the case.

A third way in which self-interest can produce good public policies is simply the flip side of much of the discussion of credit claiming in the first edition. R. Kent Weaver has argued that in an era of scarcity and difficult political choices, opportunities for credit claiming have declined, and the dangers of being blamed for undesirable conditions have increased.[42] Weaver sees blame shifting as the dynamic underlying some important congressional actions in the 1980s. Just as the experience of the Great Depression was so scathing that Congress gave up its tariff-setting powers so that it could not again be blamed for making matters worse, so the collapse of the Social Security system, or "$200 billion deficits as far as the eye can see," is sufficiently sobering that members of Congress forego their right to tinker in order to get clear of the fallout from a public policy disaster.

The general point is that members of Congress have numerous levers that can be worked to produce political gain. But that is not to say that all such activities are costless, nor that every member works every lever every minute of every day. Given their districts and their political ambitions, different members concentrate on different levers. Some members avoid some levers that other members favor. And conditions may be such that most members work a particular lever at some times, whereas most decide to avoid a particular lever at other times. When placed on the horns of a dilemma, it is not difficult to understand why members of Congress would pass off the hot potato to a bipartisan commission or agency. It is more difficult to understand why anyone would regard such behavior as public spirit in action.

I will end this section with a final clarification. The adoption of what appears to be good policy does not necessarily indicate nonpolitical, non-self-interested motives. I reject the specious argument that Congress reformed the Social Security system and therefore congressmen are public spirited. That said, I certainly do not deny that good policies may sometimes reflect good motives, or that some politicians sometimes are public spirited. The argument developed in this section addresses questions of logical inference. Those who take a less skeptical view of political life than I do must develop superior accounts premised on the primacy of public spirit over self-interest. They cannot win an intellectual debate by cataloguing rare and often ambiguous counterexamples.[43]

Clarification 6: No Conspiracies

This final clarification addresses what does seem to be malicious misreading on the part of some. *Keystone* advanced no conspiracy theory, despite Kelman's characterization of my argument as "conspiratorial speculation."[44] I quote in full the final paragraph of the original introduction:

> There is a Washington establishment. In fact, it is a hydra with each head only marginally concerned with the others' existence. These establishments are *not* malevolent, centrally directed conspiracies against the American people. Rather, they are unconsciously evolved

and evolving networks of congressmen, bureaucrats, and organized subgroups of the citizenry all seeking to achieve their own goals. Contrary to what is popularly believed, the bureaucrats are not the problem. Congressmen are. *The Congress is the key to the Washington establishment*. The Congress created the establishment, sustains it, and most likely will continue to sustain and even expand it. But I emphasize again that the disturbing aspects of the Washington establishment follow from the uncoordinated operations of the overall system, not from any sinister motivation of those who compose it. The perceptive observer can identify the actors, specify their motives, and analyze their methods of operation. But many of those in the heart of the establishment are genuinely unaware that they are members in good standing.

Chapter 12
Underemphases and New Developments

This chapter deals with topics not discussed adequately or at all in the first edition. The progress of research has revealed things that were not apparent twelve years ago, and the passage of time has thrust new developments upon us.

The Decline of Party and the Rise of Incumbency

The 1970s and 1980s saw the development of an extensive literature on the decline of American political parties. The facts are too well known to need much summary. In the 1960s opinion surveys documented a sharp jump in the number of self-identified independents.[1] Election results indicated that ticket splitting was on the rise. The influence of party professionals on nominations declined, especially at the presidential level. Technological expertise gradually began to substitute for party manpower in campaigns. And under Jimmy Carter the cohesion of the party in government eroded to a modern low point. Rather than wait for the next *realignment,* some analysts concluded that we should instead face up to a long-term period of *dealignment.*

The first edition of *Keystone* noted that the party decline literature had spawned one hypothesis about the rise of incumbency; namely, that some voters abandoned party as a guide to congressional voting and substituted incumbency. As discussed in chapter 3, this simple hypothesis appeared implausible when juxtaposed against other data. The foremost student of party decline, Walter Dean Burnham, later suggested that I had dismissed the relevance of party decline too quickly.[2] He noted that the decline of party and the rise of constituency attentiveness could be viewed as mutually compatible components of a more general account. In the light of twelve years' additional research and reflection there is good reason to believe that he is correct.

Arguably, the decline of party created a context that encouraged constituency attentiveness and made it more politically profitable; party decline in its various manifestations contributed to the motive and the opportunity for congressmen to emphasize constituency service. In the first place, as local party organizations withered, members of Congress had to replace the electoral resources that parties heretofore had provided. As discussed in chapter 7, members did so by augmenting their personal resources—staff, district offices, travel, and other allowances—and by increasing their utilization of existing resources such as the frank. Members of Congress in particular (and officeholders generally) created personal organizations to replace the party organizations that had supported earlier generations of politicians.

Electoral losers emphasize the importance of money, advertising, and blue smoke and mirrors. But media generally are not very important without a message. In the late 1950s and early 1960s, happenings in the electoral arena suggested that the times were changing and new messages were needed.[3] In 1956 Eisenhower was reelected easily while the Republicans failed to carry either house of Congress. Today's readers find nothing unusual about such an outcome, but the 1956 result was the first time in more than a hundred years that such a division had occurred, and only the second time in our political history that the party of the winning presidential candidate did not carry the House.[4] Sitting congressmen and prospective candidates probably noticed this unusual occurrence. In 1960 the candidate of the putative majority party barely won; moreover, Kennedy lost a majority of the nation's House districts and ran behind 243 of 265 winning Democratic representatives. Although in broad outline the election of 1964 resembled old times, major changes had in fact taken place. The Democratic stranglehold on the South was broken, and George Wallace opened cracks in the Democratic mass base that the party still strives to close. By the mid-1960s astute officeholders had reason to believe that the old party order, based on New Deal economic issues, was weakening, and that a more uncertain, individualistic future loomed.

Reasonably enough, incumbents read the electoral signals as indicating that they could not rely on an increasingly fickle electorate to support them on partisan grounds alone. Henceforth the basis for security would be more personal. The desire to create a personal record attractive to constituents had several implications. First, party cohesion would suffer as members resisted efforts to unify them in support of locally unpopular party or presidential positions. Second, the desire to foster an attractive personal image would lead some members to avoid highly controversial national issues and party associations altogether. In a time of deeply divided public opinion and significant social unrest, an emphasis on nonpartisan, nonideological constituency service has obvious attractions. In sum, the account of incumbent behavior given in the first edition fits nicely within a more general account of change in American politics.

Moreover, the more general account also incorporates the research on congressional challengers mentioned in chapter 10. Recall that contemporary challengers are typically unknown, unqualified, and (partly in consequence) underfunded. Where partisan ties in the electorate are strong, and party organizations correspondingly strong, the latter have the incentive and ability to field strong challengers. The incentive comes from the knowledge that voters will tend to support or oppose the ticket as a whole; thus, the organization (and its candidates!) wish to field the strongest possible ticket. The ability to induce strong candidates—typically incumbents of lesser offices—to make the race stems from two sources. First, the party can provide the necessary resources, thus largely relieving the candidates of financial risk. Second, in the (perhaps likely) event of a loss, the party can credibly promise to "take care" of the loser with another office or job. Thus, the candidate is relieved of much of the career risk of losing.[5] In contrast, under contemporary conditions many challengers risk financial hardship, if not ruin. And those potential challengers already holding office must decide whether the higher office is worth a gamble with their career. Small wonder that many "good" candidates today shy away from challenging incumbents and that many challengers are naïve amateurs and/or devotees of causes that lack majority appeal.

Thus, the rise of the personal advantage of incumbency dovetails nicely with the general decline of political party in the United States. There are even suggestion and some indication that a close scrutiny of electoral history would reveal other instances where incumbency waxed as party waned and vice versa.[6] Data on 1920s elections in particular shows some faint resemblance to patterns that emerged in the 1960s. On the other hand, John Alford and David Brady provide strong evidence that no *personal* advantage of House incumbents can be found prior to the 1960s.[7] Perhaps earlier periods of party decline provided sufficient motive but insufficient opportunity. After all, going home to the district was still a major undertaking for many congressmen in the 1920s.

Integrating the rise of incumbency and decline of parties arguments has one additional important implication: what the decline of party gave, a resurgence of party could take away. For more than a decade now, the national party organizations have been gaining strength. The Republicans have led the way, but the Democrats have imitated them and have closed the gap in recent years. These developments have received thorough coverage elsewhere, so only a few major features of contemporary party resurge need be sketched.[8] First, the national party committees and the congressional and senatorial campaign committees have expanded their roles in raising money for and channeling money into congressional races. Direct contributions are only part of the story; "coordinated" expenditures allow them to funnel much larger amounts of party money into races of importance to them. Though PACs receive the lion's share of attention in discussions of campaign finance, the role of party has increased significantly over the past decade. Moreover, PAC activities are not entirely independent of the parties, which can and do signal PACs about the prospects of worthy candidates. Second, the party committees have become repositories of modern campaign expertise such as polling, media usage, fund-raising, and campaign management.[9] Candidates receive information, education, and direct help from their parties. Third, in recent years the party committees have done something that has little precedent in the United States: they have intervened directly in the processes of local candidate selection, identifying credible candidates, supporting them in primaries, and making resources available to them.

Presumably, if incumbents became increasingly indebted to national party organizations, party leaders would have more leverage for producing votes in support of party or presidential programs.[10] And when cohesion increases, individual policy distinctiveness declines and party differences become more prominent. House elections would become less personal, more partisan, and more programmatic. If reformers would like to see congressional elections move in that direction, there are obvious paths to follow: do everything constitutionally possible to restrict the activities of PACs and individual contributors, and repeal laws that restrict the activities of the parties.[11] Of course, such "reforms" would probably not affect the two parties equally.[12] At present the Democrats have a weaker national party effort and greater success with PACs, so their interests conflict with those of the Republicans. Moreover, rank-and-file incumbents in either party are unlikely to see as much merit in party resurgence as presidents, party leaders, and professors.

What about Senate Elections?

Like the great majority of academic studies, the first edition of *Keystone* was a book about *Congress* that focused almost entirely on the *House of Representatives*. There are simple reasons for this imbalance in the literature. First, senators are much less accessible to academics, who are rarely members of breakfast clubs. Second, there are many fewer senators and senatorial elections, so statistical analysis of Senate elections is less illuminating. Thus, whenever it appears that patterns and processes are similar in the two bodies, researchers tend to study the House and observe that things appear to be similar in the Senate.

In chapter 3 I discussed a study of Senate elections by the late Warren Kostroski. Looking at postwar elections up to 1970, Kostroski found that the advantage of incumbency in Senate races had increased even more than in the House. Thus, it seemed reasonable to assume that similar processes were at work and that an explanation for the House would also suffice as an explanation for the Senate.

More recent elections threw cold water on that presumption. The roller-coaster pattern of Senate elections since the late 1970s contrasts sharply with the dull predictability of House results. Even given the electoral upheavals of the Reagan era, House incumbents have maintained their high reelection rates, ranging from 90 percent in 1982 to 98 percent in 1986 and 1988. In contrast, only 60 percent of Senate incumbents succeeded between 1976 and 1980. In 1982 and 1984 more than 90 percent won—a return to normalcy? But then came 1986, when only three-fourths of the running senators were reelected.

While we still lack an adequate research base, analysts agree that most Senate elections are significantly different from most House elections.[13] Reasonably enough, they appear to occupy a niche somewhere between presidential and House elections. Typically they attract serious challengers, issues and ideology are important, and they are hard-fought, visible contests. Certainly senators devote significant resources to constituency service— some are famous for it. But in general they cannot go through a campaign sounding like ombudsmen. Their personal characteristics, issue positions, and major legislative accomplishments dominate the debate.[14]

None of this should come as any great surprise. Senators are many fewer in number than representatives. Senators receive much more media attention and the media understandably enough want newsworthy material; typically that does not include Social Security checks or small pork-barrel projects.[15] Most information citizens have about House incumbents comes *from* House incumbents; senators have much less control about what is printed and said about them. Additionally, nominations for an office that is so exclusive, visible, and prestigious seldom go begging. Though the "most logical" challenger may still shy away from facing a strong incumbent, nominations generally go to someone with reasonable visibility and fund-raising potential. Thus, a much higher portion of Senate races than House races find credible challengers who get sufficient media coverage to probe the vulnerabilities in incumbents' records.

Finally, for a variety of reasons senators traffic more than representatives in broad policy questions. For one thing, election to the Senate appears to carry an almost automatic presumption that the senator is presidential material. But one cannot become a serious contender by staying close to home and taking care of business. One must show breadth and vision, which, unfortunately for senators, happens to be more dangerous than nose-to-the-grindstone home-state work. Even senators without obvious higher aspirations tend to get involved in broad policy questions that have attendant political risks. For example, despite the Senate's constitutional obligations in the realm of foreign affairs, several senators have suffered from the charge that "the Senator from Iowa has become the Senator for Africa." [16]

Thus, for a variety of reasons senators lead tougher electoral lives than representatives. [17] Possibly they are more ambitious or more willing to gamble on winning bigger prizes. Certainly they are more visible, more newsworthy, and more likely to encounter serious challenges. Issues and ideology have a more important place in their campaigns than in House campaigns. There is one similarity worth noting, however: contemporary Senate races are equally as *personal* as contemporary House races. Like representatives, senators are elected on the basis of their personal records, though the substance of that record differs. Senators are not elected as representatives of national parties, nor as spear-carriers for presidents. Since this conclusion appears to contradict the gross outlines of the 1980 and 1986 results, it deserves some elaboration.

In 1980 the Republicans gained twelve Senate seats and broke the quarter-century Democratic monopoly of Congress. A half-dozen prominent liberal Democrats were among the casualties. Together with Reagan's surprisingly impressive victory, the Senate results fueled speculation that a new era had dawned. The country had turned to the right, there was a resurgence of conservatism, liberalism was dead. As I have shown elsewhere, all of that might be true, but the Senate returns were not the place to find the evidence. [18]

First, as various commentators noted, the Republican vote was very "efficient"—with only 47.7 percent of the national vote, they won a majority by taking all of the close races in small states. Second, with a single exception, the losing liberals had narrowly prevailed in their previous reelections—in

1974, a great Democratic year. And before that they had all won in 1968 amidst the political chaos of the Vietnam era. This group of senators simply were not in tune with their respective states and had been living on borrowed time for at least six years. Whether the political currents of 1980 were gentle breezes or fierce gales did not matter; either would have toppled them.

In 1986 the situation reversed. This time the Republicans lost eight seats and control of the Senate, and commentators pronounced the end of the Reagan era. Again, that may be true, but the Senate returns are not the place to look. This time the Republicans actually did better in the national vote, capturing almost 50 percent, but they lost the close races in the small states.

So, the Reagan era began with the Republicans garnering 47.7 percent of the national Senate vote; it ended with an *increase* to 49.7 percent. The interpretations were not credible on either end. Senate races are probably the most personalized in the political system, the great majority of them are now well funded and competitive, and huge variations in the size of state electorates (compare California with Nevada, for example) makes any cross-state inferences dangerous. Whatever their obvious partisan and policy consequences, one should not look to Senate races for understanding of things that were or portents of things to come.[19]

Congressional Staffs

In a 1977 article that previewed the first edition of *Keystone,* I remarked on the significant increases in congressional staff, but could only pose the question "What are these people doing?"[20] At the time, congressional staffs had received little attention, and only fragmentary information such as that presented in chapter 7 was available. That situation has changed considerably. Painstaking research by Harrison Fox and Susan Hammond, Burdett Loomis, Samuel Patterson, Robert Salisbury and Kenneth Shepsle, and Michael Malbin, among others, has greatly expanded our knowledge of the size, shape, and duties of the staff that supports today's Congress.[21] While the main intent of this section is to consider the consequences of staff development for Congress, a few of the major trends and developments should be highlighted.[22]

Almost twenty-five thousand people are now employed by congressmen individually and collectively. The House currently employs about twelve thousand people and the Senate six thousand, with personal staff outnumbering committee staff roughly four to one in each chamber. About three thousand work in support agencies such as the Congressional Budget Office, Library of Congress, General Accounting Office, and Office of Technology Assessment, and another three thousand work for the Architect and the Capitol Police. Each representative employs an average of eighteen staff, and each senator twice as many, although the latter figure (which is pegged to state population) shows more variation. Subcommittee chairmanships, which are numerous and well spread in both House and Senate, provide many members an added complement of staff (see chapter 7).

In the first edition my main interest was in the use of personal staff for constituency service. The proportion of the staff assigned to district offices (table 5) has continued to rise, exceeding 40 percent in 1985, about triple the number assigned to the districts in 1960. And since much constituency work is carried out in Washington, the proportion of the personal staff devoted to constituency affairs surely exceeds 50 percent.[23] As discussed in chapter 10, however, even with the relative increase in the proportion of staff devoted to constituency service, the absolute increase in staff numbers gives members a much greater potential for legislative as well as constituency work. Much of the intervening research has focused on the role of staff in legislative work and raises a set of concerns that I did not anticipate in the first edition.

Scholars who have examined the subject most carefully express three concerns about the explosion in staffing. First, the ostensible justification for staff expansion is to enable Congress to cope with a burgeoning workload and to free Congress from dependence on the executive branch and private interests for its information. Unfortunately, larger staffs may not have the desired effects; indeed, they may make things worse. As Michael Malbin writes:

> Congress has failed utterly to cope with its workload. If anything, the growth of staff has made the situation worse. First, on the level of sheer numbers, more staff means more information coming in to each member's office, with more management problems as different staff aides compete for the member's time to present their own nuggets in a timely fashion. . . . Second, the problems created by large numbers are exacerbated by the staff's new roles. Increasingly, the members want aides who will dream up new bills and amendments bearing their bosses' names instead of helping the bosses understand what is already on the agenda. The result is that the new staff bureaucracy and the workload it helps create threaten to bury Congress under its own paperwork, just as surely as if the staff never existed.[24]

The problem Malbin identifies arises directly from electoral incentives. If members were primarily interested in becoming better informed about the myriad issues that come before Congress, they would assign their staff to study and research, and their personal workload surely would be lightened. But political temptations inevitably distort such an innocent world.[25] Staff can be used to enhance the image of the member; therefore, they will be used that way. This means bills and amendments, hearings and investigations that bear the member's personal stamp. Staff on the prowl for opportunities leave no stone unturned or piece of turf unplowed. Making the member look good is their principal responsibility; they do it well. But such activities contribute to information overload rather than alleviate it.

A second concern raised by staff expansion rises from the conception of Congress as a deliberate body. A major strain of American political thought views Congress as a collection of local ambassadors with varied interests and perspectives who come together and, through extensive personal interaction, gain a better understanding of the common good, as well as the particular needs and aspirations of different interests and areas.[26] Congress is democracy at its best. From this perspective, staff expansion detracts from the deliberative function of Congress. Members rush from committee meeting to committee meeting and flit back and forth between Washington and their districts. Meanwhile, the staffs deliberate, and understanding is not the goal—credit is. All too often members talk to their staffs, who talk to other members' staff, who talk to their members, who talk back to their staff, and so on and so forth up and down the chain. Members themselves complain that they have insufficient chance to get to know one another and express appreciation for opportunities to get together sans staff.

Personally, I have always found it a bit difficult to tell where deliberation ends and logrolling begins, but without taking any firm position, it certainly is fair to say that the existence of large staffs lengthens the lines of communication among members, insulates them from one another and sometimes even from their constituents, and in an overall sense isolates them to a degree not possible in the past. This is a *relative* judgment, to be sure; compared to presidents and judges, members of Congress are anything but isolated.

The third concern raised by large staffs is related to the second, but reaches to the very heart of democracy: the accountability of decision makers to the electorate. Congressional staff generally are careful not to overstep the (perceived) bounds of their authority, and they rarely function as independent entities. Nevertheless, discretion inevitably accompanies delegation. The staff act as gatekeepers, affecting the flow of information to and from members. They make judgments about what to pass on and how to present it. And while they must keep members' political interests primary as a condition of their employment, they have interests of their own as well. Malbin suggests that staff are more ideological then members, that they are more willing to listen to interests without constituencies than are members, and that their own career prospects lead them to view the legislative process a bit differently from members. For better or worse, in these and other subtle ways, perspectives of staff can differ from the perspectives of the principals whom they represent. To the extent that the staff influence outcomes, the locus of decision making moves one step away from direct electoral accountability.

Political scientists have an occupational sensitivity to arguments about electoral accountability (which is not to say that they agree about what it is), but it is difficult to see how there is any going back. Moreover, the skeptic might observe that if political scientists want to worry about electoral accountability, why not worry about bureaucrats who are several steps further removed than congressional staff? Or for that matter, why not worry about judges, who are fundamentally unaccountable policymakers?[27]

Whatever the ultimate answer to these broad questions, there is little doubt that the subject of congressional staffing deserves even more research than it has already received. What looked like an interesting new development in 1976 has obviously become an integral part of the Congress today.

Subcommittee Government

In chapter 7, I discussed the proliferation of subcommittees and the apparent devolution of collective power to component parts of the institution. Twelve years ago I expected this development to lead to a corresponding proliferation of subgovernments. To review briefly, civics-book accounts of how public policy is made often do not correspond to "normal politics." Aside from a few major issues that are important components of the president's program or the direct reflection of major societal problems, most issues do not receive the sustained attention of the president, the press, the citizenry, and majorities of Congress. Instead, for all practical purposes policy is made and implemented within subsystems composed of congressional committees with jurisdiction over, agencies with statutory responsibility for, and clienteles affected by the policy.[28] In their more extreme manifestations, subgovernments are often called "iron triangles." The incentives that support such arrangements are not difficult to identify. Committee members enjoy the opportunity to exercise great influence in a particular policy area—given the pattern of committee assignments, often an area of considerable concern to their districts. The agency receives protection and support from the committee. The clientele gains benefits from the program, and the circle closes when the clientele provides support for friendly committee members. Heterogeneity of interests across districts and states underpins the system. One congressman cares about federal water projects but not federal workers, while another congressman has the opposite concern. Both are politically better off if they implicitly trade for the right to exert disproportionate influence in the area of greater concern.

Twelve years ago it appeared logical to suppose that more subcommittees would lead to more subgovernments. I know of no research that addresses this question in a comprehensive way, but simple observation of Congress suggests that, if anything, the importance of subgovernments has declined.[29] This development appears to reflect a number of factors both internal and external to Congress.

Among the external factors, the most important appears to be the great expansion in the interest group universe. Traditional subgovernment politics was based on a harmony of interests among a small number of concerned actors. But in the past two decades interest groups have proliferated, and the old days of a committee dealing with a few friendly groups are long gone.[30] The representation of business groups in Washington has exploded as each specialized producer and trade interest has organized. They keep watch over one another, and various ''public interest'' groups keep tabs on all of them. All of this tends to bring politics out in the open. Subgovernments generally fail to thrive in the glare of publicity—their particularistic excesses are difficult to defend as anything other than special interest favoritism. A world of active public interest groups, jealous business competitors, and packs of budding investigative reporters is less hospitable to subgovernment politics than a world lacking them.

Beyond external changes, developments within Congress have made subgovernment politics more difficult and less advantageous than previously. Larry Dodd and Richard Schott argue that congressional decentralization has proceeded to such an extent that subgovernment functioning has been impaired.[31] Many modern issues, such as energy and the environment, do not mesh well with a committee structure now more than a generation old. With so many subcommittees and so many cross-cutting issues, jurisdictional conflicts among subcommittees have become common. The entrepreneurial activities of credit-seeking staff and members exacerbate the problem as they trespass on one another's turfs. Few agencies need answer to a single powerful committee any longer; rather, according to Dodd and Schott, agencies can play off their various subcommittee masters against one another and gain added discretion from the competition and conflict among their one-time masters. Again, there is little research that directly evaluates this argument, but the possibility seems real.

Another (related) reason why subgovernment politics has not expanded in contemporary Congresses lies in the general movement of congressional power from the committees to the floor. Subgovernments presume that committees are capable of discouraging or at least defeating outside attempts to intervene. But most observers believe that committees today are less powerful than was previously the case. The frequency of floor amendments is up and the role of floor majorities appears to have increased.[32] In part this may reflect the previously mentioned rise in jurisdictional conflict as aggrieved members of one committee attack the work of another. In part members may no longer be as willing to limit their political interests as they were previously; perhaps social and economic change has made congressional districts and states internally more heterogeneous and thus less receptive to members who limit their involvement. Additionally, the activities of public interest groups and ideological PACs undoubtedly make it more difficult for congressmen to defend self-imposed limitations on their involvement than it was in the past.

The previous paragraphs refer in part to large-scale political and societal changes whose full consequences are only beginning to be understood. Thus, little more than a sketch of the possibilities can be offered. But some smaller-scale institutional consequences seem reasonably clear. Being a subcommittee chair today is nothing like being a committee chair of yesteryear; indeed, being a committee chair of today is nothing like being a committee chair of yesteryear. Dividing up committee positions has divided up committee authority and opportunity as well. Ironically, "subcommittee government" may have proved so conflictual, incoherent, and unworkable that it has generated pressure to strengthen the role of parties and the party leadership.[33]

There is, however, one caveat that should be expressed prior to leaving this subject. For eight years we have lived with a divided government headed by a president who did not believe in politics-as-usual. This makes it difficult to differentiate true changes from temporary exceptions. Has subgovernment politics failed to flourish during the Reagan era because of the general reasons outlined above, or because Reagan appointees were in many cases hostile to their agencies' programs and the politics that sustained them? Does the floor appear more important for the reasons suggested above, or because it provides an arena to compile an opposition record? Would pent-up politics-as-usual reassert itself with a vengeance if one party gained unified control of the national government?

The possibility cannot be dismissed, but I tend to think that the changes outlined reflect underlying changes in our politics more than the impact of one president. When Reagan leaves, public interest groups and unconnected PACs will not disband, congressional committees will not recentralize, and entrepreneurial members and staff will not change their ways.[34] Nothing on the horizon suggests that we are likely to return to the neat and tidy world of subgovernment politics that characterized the heyday of committee government.

PACs and Other Special Interests

In the later chapters of the first edition I argued that members' efforts to service individual constituents and districts detract from the kind of political process that would serve more genuinely common interests. The general theme was the tension between particularistic local interests and more universalistic national interests. Local vs. national is not the only form of particular vs. universal, however. Most obviously, when commentators decry "special interests" that compete with more general interests, they often refer to interest groups that transcend congressional district boundaries. The explosion of PACs in the past decade highlights this observation.

The first edition did not ignore the existence of group interests, but simply made the assumption that group interests were important primarily as they were transmitted through constituents. Given the literature of the time this was a reasonable presumption. The national Chamber of Commerce was influential because of its ability to stimulate the local chambers. The national AFL-CIO was powerful because of its ability to mobilize local unions. The National Farm Bureau counted because members of Congress listened to the local bureaus. The most influential interests were those that worked through their grass-roots membership, not directly on the congressman. This remains true so far as lobbying goes, but the rapidly expanding role of political action committees in financing elections suggests that we should take a second look at the influence of groups located outside the geographic districts of members.

The acronym PAC did not appear in the first edition. For one thing, there were many fewer of them twelve years ago. Few students today appreciate how large and rapid the growth of PACs has been. In the aftermath of the Federal Election Campaign Act amendments of 1974 and the Federal Election Commission SUN-PAC decision of late 1975, there was a PAC explosion: between the mid-1970s and mid-1980s PACs increased more than sevenfold, with corporate PACs leading the way (table 13). For another thing, congressional elections in the mid-1970s were much cheaper than today, and their financing seemed a less burning issue. At any rate, reliable data on campaign financing did not become available until 1972, when the Federal Election Campaign Act took effect, and the first systematic research on money in congressional elections did not appear until the end of the decade.[35] While the PAC phenomenon was under way twelve years ago, I did not then anticipate its continued development or potential importance.

The growth of PACs could weaken district ties to members of Congress and strengthen the influence of interest groups not tied to specific districts. The conditional is intended here, for the evidence is inconclusive. As discussed earlier, the decline of party and the increasing importance of expensive campaign technology have forced members of Congress to seek new sources of sustenance. To some extent they have put the hit on the taxpayer to provide what they need, but most of them believe it is far from sufficient. Hence, each successive election is accompanied by reports of new fundraising records, new spending records, new most-expensive races, and, above all, new stories about the pernicious influence of money, especially

Table 13. Growth in PACs

Type	1974	1978	1982	1986
Corporate	89	784	1,467	1,744
Labor	201	217	380	384
Nonconnected	—	165	746	1,077
Other	318	487	778	952
Total	608	1,653	3,371	4,157

Source: Ornstein, Mann, and Malbin, *Vital Statistics on Congress, 1987–1988* (Washington, D.C.: American Enterprise Institute Congressional Quarterly Press), p. 103.

PAC money. And it is precisely in this last particular where we find a disjunction between the writings of journalists and reformers on the one hand, and those of academic specialists on the other. To the former, the pernicious influence of PACs is patently obvious.[36] To the latter, there are more questions than answers.[37] Journalists and reformers tend to think they know more about PACs and their influence than they do.

Let us begin with the question of most significance for the arguments in this book—the potential of PACs to weaken the close link between congressmen and their geographic constituencies. Only citizens of the district can vote, but PAC money from outside the district obviously can be used to enhance political support inside the district. How much outside PAC money flows into congressional races?

Table 14 contains breakdowns of the sources of campaign contributions in recent elections. As shown, the principal source of contributions has been and continues to be individual contributions. PAC contributions have aroused so much comment in part because of their rapid rate of growth, though they still amount to only about a third of total contributions in recent House races. As for Senate races, PAC contributions amount to only one-fifth of the total and do not show the same rapid growth as in House races.[38] Of course, these figures say nothing about the geographic location of the contributors.

Janet Grenzke has studied the geographic origination of campaign contributions to sitting House incumbents between 1977 and 1982, based on careful matching of district and contributor zip codes.[39] There are inevitable ambigu-

Table 14. Sources of Congressional Campaign Funds

	1974	1978	1982	1986
House				
Party	4%	7%	6%	4%
PACs	17	24	31	36
Individual	79	69	63	60
Senate				
Party	6	6	10	8
PACs	11	13	17	22
Individual	83	81	73	70

Source: Ornstein, Mann, and Malbin, *Vital Statistics on Congress, 1987–1988* (Washington, D.C.: American Enterprise Institute Congressional Quarterly Press), pp. 92–93.

ities in the data. A firm's PAC may be located outside the district, but perhaps its executives live within the district. An individual contributor may live outside the district, but perhaps a significant part of her business takes place within the district. For this reason Grenzke calculates proportions of contributions both within district and within state. She finds that only about half of all individual contributions originate within the district, though about four-fifths originate within the state. The proportion of contributions coming from outside the district and state declined markedly over the five-year period, however. The nonlocal tilt of PAC money is much more pronounced. Virtually all PAC contributions come from out of district, and more than four-fifths come from out of state. Again, there is a discernible trend for money to come from out-of-state sources.[40]

So the bare facts suggest that campaign contributions (PAC and otherwise) tempt congressmen to consider interests they otherwise might not consider. That temptation seems all the more real when we consider the broad contours of PAC contributions. Such contributions disproportionately flow to incumbents, to Democrats, and to representatives who hold institutional bases of power. All these are related, of course, but it is not important that they be disentangled here. What is important is simply that many corporate and trade PACs contribute to representatives whose party and political roots do not mark them as sympathetic to PAC interests.[41]

Circumstantial evidence like the preceding provides a basis for journalistic charges that PAC funding will lead members to vote for special interests rather than the general interest, or at least the interests of their districts. I would pose the question somewhat differently. The main theme of this book is that, PACs or no, congressmen rarely vote the general interest. Individual district interests *are* special interests, whose sum is *not* the national interest. Thus, the question is whether PACs lead members to substitute one set of special interests defined by money for another set defined by geography.[42] But however we pose the question, there is insufficient evidence to provide a conclusive answer.

In a nutshell, does money buy new friends, or does money reward existing friends? The distinction involves more than an "academic" question. In my teaching I have long used an exposé entitled "The Dairy Lobby Buys the Cream of the Congress."[43] Although the article deals with congressional actions in 1971, dairy industry PACs existed even then, and the analysis exemplifies simplistic thinking about this subject. Briefly, price supports generally deemed adequate were raised after a bipartisan effort in the Congress convinced Secretary of Agriculture Clifford Hardin and President Nixon to withdraw their earlier opposition. The article recounts the campaign contributions made to members of the House and Senate who supported the push for increased supports. The telltale pattern of contributions seemed to constitute a clear smoking gun—members were rewarded for services rendered. On the other hand, is it just nitpicking to point out that many members who supported the increase hailed from districts where support for farmers was a sine qua non of representation? Is it not relevant to note that a number of the principals exposed in the article represented states like Minnesota and Wisconsin with large populations of dairy cattle? Rather than believe that Hubert Humphrey was bought for $10,625, I find it easier to believe that Humphrey did what he did for the sake of Minnesota dairy farmers, who had been an important part of his coalition from the beginning. Did he and Senator William Proxmire (D., Wisconsin) and Senator Harold Hughes (D., Iowa) advance a special interest? Absolutely. Did they do it for the money? Probably not.

As discussed in the first edition, the congressional committee system allows members to advance the special interests of their districts. Members can lay claim to committee assignments relevant to their district interests, and the disproportionate power enjoyed by committees within their jurisdictions gives members opportunities to do things for their districts. If friendly PACs make contributions, so much the better. For most members the sensible political strategy is to cultivate a set of organized interests that are at least not inconsistent with the interests of their districts. By following such a strategy members will earn campaign contributions for voting as they would anyway. The evidence seems to indicate that PACs, rather than attempting to buy votes of congressmen, contribute to those who have not been hostile in the past. For their money they hope to ensure continued access and good relations with congressmen who have been friendly, and to keep friendly congressmen in office. It is simply not enough to show that corporate and trade PACs contribute to Democratic congressmen, and then rest your case; to demonstrate an illegitimate and worrisome influence, one must show further that members are behaving inconsistently with the district coalitions that elect them.

The preceding somewhat optimistic view is subject to a few qualifications. First, whatever the reality, the appearance of a Congress on the take is undesirable. My worry here is not the disillusionment of little children or idealistic citizens. Rather, the appearance of corruption will stimulate reformers, who quite possibly will make matters worse, as they often have done in the past. Second, given the members' killing schedules, any time spent raising funds is time that could probably be better spent some other way. Moreover, fund-raising is widely regarded as the most distasteful part of a politician's job. Compared to a generation ago, the job is unattractive enough without the added burden of fund-raising. Third, the all-purpose committees, such as House Ways and Means and Senate Finance, are exceptions to my generally sanguine view. With jurisdiction over federal taxes, these committees handle myriad obscure proposals that are not of obvious relevance to their members' geographic districts. Thus, on many issues the districts do not provide any policy direction, even a potential one.[44] In this situation the temptation to trim one's actions so as to accommodate a contributor is probably greater than when a congressman's committee assignment casts up issues of clear and obvious relevance to his district. Certainly, members of the money committees receive generous campaign contributions from PACs.[45]

Still, even this suspicious pattern may reflect nothing so simple as payment for services rendered. Whether money follows votes or vice versa is one of those chicken-and-egg problems that as yet has no clear answer. Political scientists have attacked the subject with complex statistical procedures, but to date the results are inconclusive. None of the studies on the question of whether money buys or follows votes can be considered definitive.

As the preceding discussion suggests, I am not one of those who believe we are living in an era of unprecedented political corruption. A familiarity with previous eras, such as the late nineteenth century, makes such charges untenable on their face. But even restricting our attention to the modern period suggests that things are not so bad as some charge. What we think of as plain and simple corruption is probably as uncommon in today's Congress as it has ever been. If corruption sometimes seems rampant, it is probably because the process is more exposed today than ever before. Contribution and expenditure figures are public. Congress operates ''in the sunshine.'' Investigative reporters ply their trade. All of this too often gives the appearance of corruption; but generally it is only appearance. No, the problem with Congress is more serious. The problem with Congress is that congressmen conscientiously, openly, and as a matter of electoral survival assiduously service the special interests of their districts. And in the absence of the coordinating forces of strong parties or presidential leadership, the general interest of the United States gets lost in the shuffle.

Chapter 13
Looking Back and Looking Ahead

The first edition of this book ended on a pessimistic note. The incentives that had supported the particularistic, disorganized national policy-making process of the 1970s seemed stronger to me than any countervailing incentives, existing or easily imaginable. Without high hopes I did mention two possible avenues for improvement. First, there was the possibility that congressmen would find their new, more electorally secure but more locally oriented life less personally satisfying than an electorally riskier but more nationally oriented life. Having swung the electoral pendulum to the extreme that it had reached in the late 1970s, perhaps congressmen themselves would swing it back. There were some hopeful signs in the late 1970s. Congressional retirement rates had increased, and it was not only the aged and the electorally threatened who were calling it quits. Subsequent research revealed that job dissatisfaction was an important reason given for retirement, especially by those who might otherwise appear to be in the congressional prime of life.[1] Moreover, the average age of members decreased (though it has gone up again in recent years), average educational achievement went up, and increasingly members appeared to have personal policy interests they wished to pursue. These and other indicators lead most Washington observers to judge that the overall quality of today's members is the highest ever.

Unfortunately, none of the preceding appears to have greatly altered the character of the Congress. As discussed in chapters 10 and 12, the district presence of members is as pronounced as ever, the struggle for credit and turf is as fierce as ever, and the particularistic impulse remains the animating spirit of the institution. It is as difficult as ever to line up the troops in support of a presidential or party program that embodies a coherent approach to a national or international problem.[2] Better members? Apparently yes. Better results? Apparently no.

One reason that individualism and particularism have not declined lies in the electoral conditions that are the principal subject of this book. Objectively, incumbents win by bigger margins, on average, and have near-universal victory rates (98 percent in 1986 and 1988). But by all indications their psychological sense of security has not increased.[3] Indeed, the foremost student of congressional elections believes that it has decreased; Gary Jacobson contends that members today "run scared" to a greater degree than they did when electoral margins were smaller.[4] The explanation for this seeming contradiction probably lies in the developments discussed in chapter 12.

Twenty years ago political observers freely used the terms *safe* and *marginal* when referring to congressional districts. For the most part their judgments reflected the underlying distribution of party strength in districts. A safe district was one that was safe for a particular party, whoever its candidate was (within reason, of course). Today, *safe* and *marginal* are less useful terms. Judgments of safety are more contingent and less reflective of party strength. To say that a seat is safe generally means that it is safe for a particular incumbent so long as that incumbent avoids major political errors and continues to do the things that have produced comfortable margins in the past.[5] Electoral support rooted in party strength apparently was a more dependable form of support than today's support built on personal effort. At the least, partisan support was less under one's personal control, and therefore there was less point to being obsessively preoccupied with it. Today's incumbents win more but enjoy it less because of the weighty knowledge that *everything* rests on their shoulders; they walk the electoral world alone. I am not trying to inspire sympathy for incumbents—obviously, challengers are more in need of it. Rather, the point is that more energetic, more educated, and more policy-interested congressmen can still be forced by circumstances to place as much emphasis on particularism as their less personally impressive predecessors.

So, the hope for an internally generated transformation of the congressional policy-making process was apparently for naught.[6] Most congressmen are fully aware of the problems with Congress, and many are quite thoughtful when discussing them, but electoral imperatives continue to stand in the way of significant change.

The conclusion to the first edition pointed out a second avenue that could lead national politics to a higher level. This was the possibility that the electorate might end-run the Congress by electing an "outsider" president who would throw sand in the gears of congressional politics-as-usual.[7] Jimmy Carter was the one I had in mind; Ronald Reagan was the one we got.

Carter's campaign, of course, popularized the term *Washington establishment*. From the standpoint of the argument in this book, Carter had the right impulses. He was, however, something less than a virtuoso politician.[8] Both points are well illustrated by one of Carter's first presidential actions—a proposal to eliminate nineteen economically and/or environmentally unsound water projects from the budget. In the larger scheme of things not a great deal of money was involved, but water projects were the quintessential example of congressional particularism, the embodiment of the "pork barrel."[9] Carter's action was a dagger aimed at the heart of Congress, as the anguished and angry reactions of his partisans in Congress demonstrated.[10] Ultimately, nine projects were killed at a cost of much congressional goodwill. Whatever the symbolic impact of this budgetarily insignificant outcome, many believe that the imbroglio contributed greatly to Carter's subsequent poor relations with Congress.

At any rate, the outsider from Plains, Georgia, was defeated by a candidate who was even more a Washington outsider: the leader of the militant wing of a party that had fought the Democratic programs of the past half century. Some of the conditions attendant to Reagan's election were highly consistent with my description of an outsider president in the first edition of *Keystone*. In particular, while majorities of the citizenry expressed disenchantment with government regulation and taxation in general, with a few exceptions there were no majorities in favor of deregulating particular areas or cutting specific programs.[11] This is exactly what one would expect from a system that satisfies particularistic demands by a pattern of generalized logrolling. Each constituency is satisfied seriatim, but the end result is that all end up feeling that government is costing too much and is too intrusive. At such a time they may vote for a "cooperative solution," a president who promises sacrifice, but sacrifice that will be shared fairly by all. The logic is analogous to that of an arms race: parties striving for more might all be willing to settle for less if they could be sure that the competing parties would do likewise.[12]

Despite some noteworthy first-year successes on the composition of the budget, the Reagan administration soon found the limits of the mutual denial strategy. After the initial rounds of cuts, further reductions became difficult or impossible. For one thing, particular constituencies became desperate, which in turn heightened the intensity of their political activity. For another thing, generalized sentiment for less government spending naturally declined after the initial cuts were made and after affected constituencies communicated their desperation. In addition, lavish spending (later revealed to be egregiously wasteful) in the defense sector provided an unfavorable contrast with domestic belt-tightening. As a result of these trends in sentiment, by

1983 particularistic support for government activities was able to hold off generalized sentiment for further reductions in government activity. A disappointed David Stockman recounts that, among other things, conservatives underestimated the extent to which the American people supported the welfare state.[13] Probably he is correct. But the perception of shared sacrifice is a necessary condition for the success of the mutual denial strategy, and one thing the Reagan administration had trouble with from the beginning was the perception that some elements of the Republican coalition were fattening on the sacrifices of none-too-affluent citizens—"fairness" was a major theme in the 1982 elections. Throw in some unwise attacks on generally popular programs, most obviously environmental regulation, and the unraveling of the mutual sacrifice strategy is not hard to understand.

To be sure, Ronald Reagan has had an enormous impact on congressional politics. It is only a slight exaggeration to say that he created a government of confrontation and continuing resolution. Outside of a few major areas like Social Security, Medicare, and agriculture subsidies, the domestic sector has been pared back. By creating large deficits, Reagan imposed constraints on congressional tendencies for years to come—unless, of course, the Congress musters the political courage to raise taxes enough to eliminate the deficits and allow for new spending. Congressmen have struggled to keep program structures intact, even as funding dwindles.[14] Some programs have been killed,[15] but on the whole Congress has dragged its heels, kicked and screamed, and fought a holding action for the day when the Reagan aberration would pass, when old programs could be nourished back to health and new ones birthed. But the aberration continues, it now appears.

The deficit, incidentally, provides an apparent counterexample to much of what has just been said. In the 1980s it has been the *Congress* that has demanded a balanced budget. It has been the *Congress* that has demanded that taxes be raised. Obviously, such demands are out of Congress's traditional character. Under one interpretation, Congress has risen above its distributive proclivities and now stands as the responsible voice of the national interest. Perhaps. But there is another interpretation more in keeping with the traditional character of Congress. One need not be a devotee of conspiracy theories to accept Senator Daniel P. Moynihan's (D., New York) charge that the Reagan deficits were at least in part a conscious strategy to tie the hands of Congress and the Democratic party long after Reagan passed from the scene.[16]

What the Democrats in particular, and Congress in general, now realize is that Reagan created for them a problem of major proportions. In order to fund new programs, or increase the funding for existing ones, they must raise significant new revenues. Before new programs can be funded, the deficits must first be greatly reduced, else hypersensitive financial markets will react badly and the weight of informed opinion will descend on Congress. By blind accident or shrewd intention, the Reagan administration created a situation in which Congress could act out its normal tendencies in the long run only by acting as the responsible guardian of the national interest in the short run. Of course, suspicion about the purity of congressional motives should not prevent us from applauding congressional actions when such actions are meritorious. As discussed in chapter 11, that is the primary concern of political engineering—to structure institutional arrangements so that they generate acceptable outcomes from less-than-laudable motives.

A One-Party House of Representatives

Chapter 2 set out the reasons why vanishing marginals and incumbency advantages deserve attention. Party competition, with the threat and actuality of electoral replacement, traditionally has been viewed as the key to responsive government. Thus, there is a natural concern that as competition declines, responsiveness will follow. In the light of twelve years' research and experience, how much of this concern is justified?

Well, there is both good news and bad news to report. As noted earlier in this chapter, there is no evidence that contemporary congressmen are any less responsive *to their districts* than were those of earlier generations. In fact, today's members have a near obsessive preoccupation with keeping in touch: they travel, poll, mail, and in other ways keep their fingers on the district pulse. And no matter how electorally secure they may seem to outside observers, today's members run scared and take nothing for granted. This is the good news.

The bad news is that there is more to electoral responsiveness than keeping closely attuned to one's district. Indeed, the overarching theme of this work is that responsiveness in that narrow sense can impede responsiveness in a larger sense. In chapter 2 I discussed the importance of marginal districts for enabling Congress *as an institution* to respond to changes in *national* sentiment. Historically, marginal districts were the battleground on which majority control of Congress was decided. If they were to disappear and all members of Congress were to come from safe districts, then by definition

Congress would never change, except as a result of random, nonpolitical factors such as the deaths and retirements of members.

Evidently, many commentators believe that something of this sort has now come to pass. For the third consecutive presidential election the Republicans have taken more than forty states without coming close to capturing the House. The House seems to have become a Democratic preserve whose composition is impervious to the organizational efforts of the Republican party and the coattails of victorious Republican presidents.[17] Before proceeding to the larger implications of this development, it is important to have a clear understanding of how it has come about.

The developments discussed in this book have greatly eroded the historical connection between presidential and congressional outcomes. When Dwight Eisenhower was reelected president in 1956 without a majority in either house of Congress, it was only the second time in American history that such an outcome had occurred. Since then, we have seen such outcomes in 1968, 1972, and 1988. Indeed, before 1956 the party of the victorious presidential candidate had failed to carry the House on only one occasion (excluding the ambiguous 1876 outcome). Since 1956 it has happened six times. The historically unprecedented has become the contemporary norm.

The strength of the connection between presidential and congressional outcomes depends on two links (fig. 4). First, there is a link between the *vote* for both offices when partisanship, national conditions, or national issues lead voters to support presidential and congressional candidates of the same party. Second, there is a link between changes in the congressional vote and *seats* won or lost by the presidential party when the vote changes make the difference in marginal districts. Popular discussions of "coattails" often conflate these distinct linkages, but the vote link and the seat link are each important.

As the marginals vanished, the seat link naturally weakened. To illustrate, assume that a popular president produces a 3 percent across-the-board in-

Figure 4. Links between Presidential and Congressional Outcomes

presidential vote ⟶ congressional vote
                                          ↓
                              congressional seats

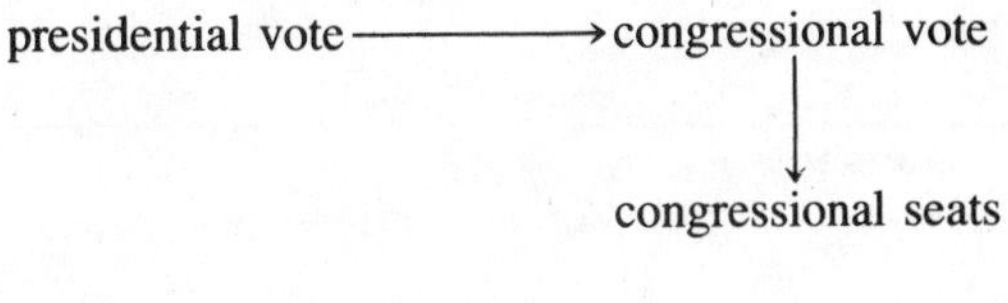

crease in the vote for his party's congressional candidates. Then, other things being equal, any opposition seat held by a margin of less than 3 percent switches to the victorious president's party. If there are no such seats, no *seats* are gained, despite the vote gain. Clearly, an electoral context with many marginals offers more favorable prospects for seat gains than a context with few marginals. (Compare 1948 with 1972 in figure 3.)

A measure called the ''swing ratio'' traditionally has been used to represent the relationship between vote changes and seat changes. The swing ratio gives the percentage gain in a party's seats that accompanies a 1 percent gain in its vote.[18] As the marginals declined, the swing ratio for U.S. national elections has declined correspondingly.[19] From a 1946–64 level of about 2.3, the swing ratio has fallen to about 1.4 in the post-1964 period. The implications of this change are most dramatically suggested by a hypothetical rerunning of history. What would congressional outcomes have been if the pre-1964 swing ratio had been in effect throughout the post-1964 period of Republican presidential hegemony?

If the marginals had not declined in number and congressional elections had remained as susceptible to national tides as they were a generation ago, then, all other things being equal, the Republicans would have taken majorities of House seats five times since the mid-1960s (table 15). Such exercises

Table 15. Republican Seats in the House

Year	Actual Number	Number Predicted under 1946–64 Conditions
1966	187	*223
1968	192	*238
1970	180	166
1972	192	*223
1974	144	157
1976	143	185
1978	158	191
1980	192	*241
1982	166	203
1984	182	*233
1986	177	206

*Predicted Republican majority

Source: Ansolabehere, Brady, and Fiorina, "The Marginals Never Vanished?"

must be viewed cautiously, since all other things may not have been equal. But table 15 pointedly suggests the significance of the vanishing marginals for Republican prospects of combining congressional majorities with presidential victories.

But Republican readers should recall a simple fact before allowing table 15 to stoke their outrage. Not since 1952 have Republican candidates received more votes for Congress than Democrats. Thus, while the electoral system has not given them the majorities that it previously would have, and while it has not given them seats in proportion to their vote (most notably, 48 percent in 1980), it has not denied them control of the House when they have won a national majority of the vote. This brings us back to the vote linkage in figure 4.

In the past two decades there have been major gaps between the votes recorded by Republican presidential and congressional candidates. In 1984, for example, Ronald Reagan received almost 59 percent of the vote, while Republican congressional candidates received only 47 percent. Contrast this with 1964 when Lyndon Johnson received 61 percent of the vote and Democratic congressional candidates received 57 percent.

The increased gap between presidential and congressional vote totals reflects the increased personalization of the congressional vote. As partisanship has declined, and as congressmen have emphasized their personal issue stands and personal service records, voting for the two offices has become increasingly independent. If a major recession occurs, voters hold the president responsible, but they are less likely to visit their frustration on the members of his party in Congress. Similarly, if the Republicans run an especially popular presidential candidate, Republican congressional candidates are not so likely to gain as in the past. And when the Democrats run an especially unpopular candidate, Democratic congressional candidates do not suffer as they once would have. Thus, not only does the declining swing ratio result in a lower Republican seat gain when they score a vote gain, but the increased personalization of the vote means that vote gains scored at the presidential level do not translate into vote gains at the congressional level. The result is the large gap between the vote totals of Nixon, Reagan, and Bush, and those of Republican congressional candidates who ran with them.

What are the prospects for Republican control of Congress any time soon? Slim or none is the obvious response. Wholesale changes in party control of House seats requires a nationalization of House elections sufficient to weaken drastically the large personal vote that now exists. While national party revival (discussed in chapter 12) carries some prospect of enhancing the national component of House elections, few observers expect such developments to proceed far enough to give a Republican president a reasonable chance of carrying the House.

So, Democratic congressional majorities are likely to persist, whatever happens at the presidential level. When important features of national politics began to change in the late 1950s and early 1960s, Democratic congressional candidates were among the first to note the changes and to adapt their behavior. Both the 1964 marginals (most of whom survived the party's 1966 losses) and the 1974 "Watergate babies" were among the pioneers in the new style of entrepreneurial politics. The political acumen of these politicians is reflected in the Democratic House majorities that have persisted while the party's presidential wing has stumbled from one failure to another.

Is the One-Party House Stagnant and Unresponsive?

"How is it that our House has ossified into a permanent Democratic majority—a smug, self-satisfied institution largely unanswerable to the changing needs of the American people?"—Outgoing Republican National Committee Chair Frank Fahrenkopf

That the House has become the political preserve of the Democratic party cannot be denied. But does unbroken partisan control mean that the House has become stagnant and unresponsive? Republicans, like Fahrenkopf, will respond with an aggrieved yes, while Democrats will vigorously dispute such charges. More disinterested observers will offer a more qualified answer.[20]

The most reasonable thing to say is that continued Democratic control of the House *dampens* its responsiveness to political change. After observing the House in 1981, it is difficult to argue that Reagan could have gotten a great deal more if the Republicans had won a narrow majority. True, the defection of southern Democrats whose districts had gone heavily for Reagan was the key. Northern Democrats formed a united front against the Reagan budget and tax cuts. Still, the Democratic alternatives they supported would themselves have been considered unthinkable two years earlier.[21] The party as a whole acted as if it had detected a shift in the wind and positioned itself accordingly. Similarly, it is hard to argue that the 1986 tax bill would have looked much different if Republicans had controlled both houses of Congress. Democrats thought there was political mileage in tax simplification, or at least feared that they would be blamed for opposing it.

On the other hand, Republican Houses probably would have given Reagan a somewhat easier time on defense spending and "Star Wars" in his second term, and no doubt Republican Houses would have been more receptive to aid for the Nicaraguan *contras*. Undoubtedly, too, a few more government programs would have met their ends. On the whole, though, the picture is not that of a House locked in the 1970s, let alone the 1950s. The House slowed the pace and moderated the extent of change during the 1980s; it did not stop change altogether.

Still, one may worry that there is more to political change than the preceding paragraph covers. For one thing, the parties have characteristic biases. Both may agree that homelessness or child care are problems, but to the extent that one party continuously controls the House, the other party's proposed solutions will get short shrift.[22] Take social welfare policies, for example, During the 1988 campaign Republicans disparaged Democratic "budget-busting" policies, and Democrats hooted at the Republicans' "thousand points of light." Democrats talk compassion, Republicans talk incentives. Democrats emphasize direct service provision, Republicans emphasize favorable by-products of prosperity. Democratic solutions pay the salaries of people who tend to be Democrats or will become so out of gratitude or dependence. Republican solutions make profits for entrepreneurs who tend to be Republicans or will become so after they have "made it on their own." The choice of public policies is rarely a dispassionate search for the technically best solution to some societal problem. Political considerations are always important and often dominate.

Thus, to the extent that Democrats control the House, the national system will have a conservative (small *c*) bias that will favor the kinds of public policies enacted by Democratic Congresses of the past. This bias against innovation will be reinforced to the degree that Democratic congressmen interpret their continued majorities as a popular mandate to "temper" or "balance" the policies of Republican presidents.

Divided Government

At several points I have remarked on the unprecedented degree to which contemporary American voters have divided control of our national institutions between the parties. Arguably, the emergence of a two-tier system in which Republican presidential majorities coexist with Democratic congressional majorities is the single most important feature of contemporary politics. Throughout most of our history elections have been the mechanism that partially overcame the constitutional separation of powers. Now elections vigorously reinforce the constitutional division. In 1989, our constitutional bicentennial year, this theme seems an appropriate one with which to conclude this book.

In designing our national system, the framers walked a fine line. On the one hand, they wished to create a government strong enough to maintain internal order, provide national defense, and uphold a system of rules and rights that would allow a national economy to develop. These were important things governments could do *for* their citizens. But through most of human history, most governments had oppressed their populations; governments were best known for what they did *to* their citizens. Hence, the framers sought to construct a government that was strong enough, but not too strong: "You must first enable the government to control the governed; and in the next place oblige it to control itself."[23] The solution they adopted was to grant great power to the federal government, but to distribute and blend that power among the separate institutions, so that they would check and balance one another.[24]

Words on paper would not be sufficient to guarantee the needed checking and balancing, however. "Parchment barriers" had to be reinforced by the most dependable of all motives: self-interest. "Ambition must be made to counteract ambition. The interest of the man must be connected with the constitutional rights of the place."[25] And the principal means of insuring that conflict of ambitions and interests was the system of separate elections established by the Constitution. Public officials would be elected at different times, by different constituencies, for different reasons.

Two hundred years of freedom is no small accomplishment. The framers indeed built well. Ironically, however, periods of great accomplishment in American politics have been periods in which the normal operation of the constitutional separation of powers is transcended. When historians rank the great presidents, they name Jefferson, Lincoln, and Franklin Roosevelt, not Pierce, Taft, and Coolidge. But a look at the "great" presidencies shows that one of their common characteristics is that strong, partisan coalitions unified the national institutions that the constitution puts asunder. These coalitions captured and held the presidency and both houses of Congress, filled the judiciary with appointees who would uphold their political actions, and in more recent times staffed the bureaucracy with appointees who extended and defended the coalition's program. During Jefferson's presidency the opposing Federalist party began to disintegrate, and the Jeffersonian coalition ruled unchallenged for a quarter-century. Lincoln's Republicans had undivided control of national institutions for fourteen years. The same was true for Roosevelt and the New Deal coalition. Successive electoral victories resulted in unbroken political control that enabled the victorious coalitions to institutionalize their political victories by injecting them deep within our formal institutions.[26]

Obviously, the post–World War II era is very different. No one can say whether any of the Republican presidents who served might have gone down as "greats" had they only had Republican Congresses throughout their administrations. But, for better or worse, we can say that none of them really had the opportunity.[27] And, as discussed earlier in this chapter, the situation is not likely to change.

So, as the century draws to a close, the constitutional design is alive and well. Separate institutions share power. Ambition counteracts ambition. For all the reasons discussed in this book, separate and independent national elections buttress the formal demarcations established by the Constitution. To a reader whose principal concern is governmental tyranny, I say, "Sleep well, you have little to fear." But for readers whose principal concern is the greenhouse effect or any of the other numerous, large-scale problems that beset the world, tossing and turning is understandable. No big changes are in sight.

Notes

Preface to the Second Edition

1. In the late 1980s polls generally show Congress with a favorability rating in the neighborhood of 35 percent, give or take 5 percent.

2. Briefly, Reeves attacks Senate Majority Leader Robert Byrd's ineffectiveness; Senator Edward Kennedy's bill of attainder against his critic, publisher Rupert Murdoch; Senator Daniel Inouye's much-publicized favor for a campaign contributor; Representative Charles Wilson's petty budgetary retaliation against the DIA; and Speaker O'Neill's parochial vision. See "Smug, Local-Minded Congress Sells Out U.S.," *San Jose Mercury News,* Jan. 6, 1988.

3. David Broder, "Housecleaning Is Needed," *San Jose Mercury News,* June 1, 1988, p. 11B.

4. See, for example, Roger Davidson and Walter Oleszek, *Congress and Its Members,* 2d ed. (Washington, D.C.: Congressional Quarterly Press, 1985), esp. chap. 16; and Gary Jacobson, *The Politics of Congressional Elections,* 2d ed. (Boston: Little, Brown, 1987), esp. chaps. 7–8.

5. Lawrence Dodd, "A Theory of Congressional Cycles," in Gerald Wright, Leroy Rieselbach, and Lawrence Dodd, eds., *Congress and Policy Change* (New York: Agathon, 1986), pp. 3–44.

6. Arthur Maass, *Congress and the Common Good* (New York: Basic Books, 1983).

7. Review by Jones in *Capitol Studies* 6 (1979): 59. For a more typical positive, if qualified, reaction, see Eric Uslaner's review in the *American Political Science Review* 72 (Sept. 1978): 1,058–59.

8. However, *Keystone* was the cowinner of the *Washington Monthly*'s annual book award. This magazine can fairly be described as in the muckraking tradition.

9. Additionally, the book criticized the "New Deal style of government." Today's students may not appreciate the partisan significance of that criticism in 1976, given that in the 1980s Democrats have often taken the lead in attacking New Deal ideas and programs. In 1976, however, the criticism was naturally taken as anti-Democratic.

10. Michael M. Uhlmann, "Congress and the Welfare State: The Electoral Connection," *Commonsense* 1 (Fall 1978): 15–26.

11. Steven Kelman, *Making Public Policy* (New York: Basic Books, 1987), p. 233.

Introduction to Part One

1. Actually this strategy appears new only on the presidential level; congressmen have been following it for years. See Richard Fenno, "If, As Ralph Nader Says, Congress Is 'the Broken Branch,' How Come We Love Our Congressmen So Much?" in Norman Ornstein, ed., *Congress in Change* (New York: Praeger, 1975), pp. 277–87.

2. Some psychologists might reply that the mass public "needs" conspiratorial explanations—that ordinary citizens are incapable of comprehending a complex political reality. I disagree. Our citizens and our politicians have been the subjects of too much psychological analysis in recent years. We would do well to focus on the simple, objective explanations for political reactions and events, rather than to seize upon romantic, imaginative, but typically fictitious psychological theories. Compare, for example, the explanations of McCarthyism propounded by sociologists in Daniel Bell, ed., *The Radical Right* (New York: Doubleday, 1964), with those advanced by political scientists such as Nelson Polsby in "Toward an Explanation of McCarthyism," *Political Studies* 8 (1960): 250–71.

Chapter 1. The Case of the Vanishing Marginals

1. For analyses of the myths and realities surrounding the seniority system see Raymond Wolfinger and Joan Hollinger, "Safe Seats, Seniority, and Power in Congress," in Robert Peabody and Nelson Polsby, eds., *New Perspectives on the House of Representatives*, 2d ed. (Chicago: Rand McNally, 1969), pp. 55–77; Barbara Hinckley, *The Seniority System in Congress* (Bloomington: Indiana University Press, 1971).

2. The figures for the House are a bit on the high side of 90 percent, while those for the Senate are a bit on the low side. See Charles Jones, *Every Second Year* (Washington, D.C.: Brookings Institution, 1967); Warren Kostroski, "Party and Incumbency in Post-War Senate Elections: Trends, Patterns, and Models," *American Political Science Review* 68 (1973): 1,213–34.

3. Morris P. Fiorina, David W. Rohde, and Peter Wissel, "Historical Change in House Turnover" in Ornstein, *Congress in Change*, pp. 24–57; H. Douglas Price, "Congress and the Evolution of Legislative 'Professionalism'," ibid., pp. 2–23; Nelson Polsby, "The Institutionalization of the U.S. House of Representatives," *American Political Science Review* 62 (1968): 144–68.

4. James S. Young, *The Washington Community* (New York: Harcourt, Brace and World, 1966).

5. For those unfamiliar with the details of the 1909–11 revolt, some general

background might be helpful. In the decades following the Civil War, a succession of strong speakers (in both parties) including Blaine, Randall, Keifer, Carlisle, "Czar" Reed, and "Boss" Cannon centralized power in the office of the Speaker. Their power rested on such tangibles as control of the committee assignment process, the power of recognition, and dominance of the Rules Committee, and perhaps on such intangibles as ideological support for strong party government. Speaker Cannon (1903–11) pushed the powers of his office to their utmost at a time when members of the House were increasingly less willing to accept arbitrary leadership. Cannon ruthlessly manipulated committee assignments and other formal powers to whip his party into line behind the program of the "regular" wing of the party. Eventually time ran out on him. The 1908 election weakened the regular wing of the party and strengthened the "progressive" wing, and in 1909 a loose coalition of progressive Republicans and Democrats managed to circumscribe the Speaker's heretofore unlimited right of recognition. In 1910 the same coalition struck a major blow, expanding the Rules Committee, removing the Speaker from it, and giving to the House as a whole the power to select the members of the committee. Later that year the Democrats won control of the House and, in organizing the Congress in 1911, gave to the House as a whole the power to assign its members to committees. Seniority soon became an automatic, nearly inviolable rule for choosing the committee leadership. The net result of the revolt was to give to the rank-and-file membership of Congress the ability to shape their own political futures. No longer could they be forced to cast a vote that might cripple them in their district; no longer could their internal base of influence be removed at the displeasure of the Speaker. The modern House—a decentralized body of career politicians answerable only to their districts—dates from the events of 1909–11. For more extended discussions see Charles Jones, "Joseph G. Cannon and Howard W. Smith: An Essay on the Limits of Leadership in the House of Representatives," *Journal of Politics* 30 (1968): 617–46; Nelson Polsby, Miriam Gallagher, and Barry Rundquist, "The Growth of the Seniority System in the U.S. House of Representatives," *American Political Science Review* 63 (1969): 787–807; and Kenneth Shepsle, *The Giant Jigsaw Puzzle: Democratic Committee Assignments in the Modern House* (Chicago: University of Chicago Press, 1978).

6. David Mayhew, "Congressional Elections: The Case of the Vanishing Marginals," *Polity* 6 (1974): 295–317.

7. In the most recent election unofficial returns indicate a continuation of these trends. Only thirteen incumbents went down to defeat. Using the 55 percent rule of thumb, over 80 percent of the 1976 winners would be classified as safe, including fifty-four of the seventy-eight-person Democratic "Watergate class" who sought reelection.

Chapter 2. The Marginal District

1. For a more extended discussion of marginal districts, see Morris P. Fiorina, *Representatives, Roll Calls, and Constituencies* (Lexington, Mass.: D.C. Heath, 1974), passim.

2. Herbert Asher and Herbert Weisberg, "Voting Change in Congress," *American Journal of Political Science* 22 (May 1978): 391–425.

3. These data are drawn from Fiorina, *Representatives, Roll Calls, and Constituencies,* chap. 5.

4. Ibid.

Chapter 3. The Vanishing Marginals

1. On religion in 1960 see Philip Converse, "Religion and Politics: The 1960 Election," in Angus Campbell et al., *Elections and the Political Order* (New York: Wiley, 1966), pp. 96–124. On the New Deal cleavages in 1964 and race throughout the 1960s, see Gerald Pomper, *Voters' Choice* (New York: Dodd, Mead, 1975).

2. In 1962 the Supreme Court handed down the original "one man, one vote" decision in Baker v. Carr. This decision struck down the Tennessee apportionment for the state legislature on the ground that it violated the equal protection clause of the Fourteenth Amendment. The court extended its decision to Congress in Wesberry v. Sanders in 1964.

3. Edward R. Tufte, "The Relationship between Seats and Votes in Two-Party Systems," *American Political Science Review* 67 (1973): 540–54; idem, "Communication," *American Political Science Review* 68 (1974): 211–13.

4. John A. Ferejohn, "On the Decline in Competition in Congressional Elections," *American Political Science Review* 71 (1977): 166–76.

5. Charles Bullock, "Redistricting and Congressional Stability, 1962–1972," *Journal of Politics* 37 (1975): 569–75; Albert Cover, "One Good Term Deserves Another: The Advantage of Incumbency in Congressional Elections," *American Journal of Political Science* 21 (Aug. 1977): 523–42.

6. Robert S. Erikson, "The Advantage of Incumbency in Congressional Elections," *Polity* 3 (1971): 395–405; idem, "Malapportionment, Gerrymandering, and Party Fortunes in Congressional Elections," *American Political Science Review* 66 (1972): 1,234–1,355.

7. Donald Stokes and Warren Miller, "Party Government and the Saliency of Congress," *Public Opinion Quarterly* 26 (1962): 531–46.

8. Angus Campbell et al., *The American Voter* (New York: Wiley, 1960).

9. Stokes and Miller, "Party Government and the Saliency of Congress."

10. Norman Vie, Sidney Verba, and John Petrocik, *The Changing American Voter* (Cambridge, Mass.: Harvard University Press, 1976).

11. Kevin Phillips, *The Emerging Republican Majority* (New York: Anchor, 1970); Walter Burnham, *Critical Elections and the Mainsprings of American Politics* (New York: Norton, 1970).

12. Walter D. Burnham and William Chambers, eds., "Party Systems and the Political Process," *The American Party Systems,* 2d ed. (New York: Oxford University Press, 1975), pp. 308–57; Erikson, "Malapportionment, Gerrymandering, and Party Fortunes in Congressional Elections"; Ferejohn, "On the Decline of Competition in Congressional Elections."

13. Arthur Miller, "Political Issues and Trust in Government: 1964–1970," *American Political Science Review* 68 (1974): 951–72.

14. U.S. Congress, Senate, Committee on Government Operations, "Confidence and Concern: Citizens View American Government," Dec. 3, 1973, Hearing.

15. Kostroski, "Party and Incumbency in Post-War Senate Elections."

Chapter 5. The Rise of the Washington Establishment

1. Henry David Thoreau, *Walden* (London: Walter Scott, n.d.), p. 72.

2. For a more extended discussion of the electoral motivation, see Fiorina, *Representatives, Roll Calls, and Constituencies,* chap. 2; and David R. Mayhew, *Congress: The Electoral Connection* (New Haven: Yale University Press, 1974).

3. For a discussion of the goals of bureaucrats, see William Niskanen, *Bureaucracy and Representative Government* (Chicago: Aldine-Atherton, 1971).

4. The traditional pork barrel is the subject of an excellent treatment by John Ferejohn. See his *Pork Barrel Politics: Rivers and Harbors Legislation, 1947– 1968* (Stanford: Stanford University Press, 1974).

5. Charles Clapp, *The Congressman: His Job As He Sees It* (Washington, D.C.: Brookings Institution, 1963), p. 84.

6. Richard Fenno, *The Power of The Purse* (Boston: Little, Brown, 1966); Aaron Wildavsky, *The Politics of the Budgetary Process,* 2d ed. (Boston: Little, Brown, 1974).

7. Clapp, *The Congressman: His Job As He Sees It,* p. 84.

8. "Hays Improves Rapidly from Overdose," *Los Angeles Times,* June 12, 1976, part 1, p. 19. Similarly, Congressman Robert Leggett (D., Calif.) won reelection in 1976 even amid revelations of a thirteen-year bigamous relationship and rumors of other affairs and improprieties. The *Los Angeles Times* wrote:

Because of federal spending, times are good here in California's 4th Congressional District, and that is a major reason why local political leaders in both parties, as well as the man on the street, believe that Leggett will still be their congressman next year. . . .

Leggett has concentrated on bringing federal dollars to his district and on acting as an ombudsman for constituents having problems with their military pay or Social Security or GI benefit checks. He sends out form letters to parents of newborn children congratulating them.

Traditionally, personal misbehavior has been one of the few shoals on which incumbent congressmen could founder. But today's incumbents have so entrenched themselves by personal service to constituents that even scandal does not harm them mortally. See David Johnson, "Rep. Leggett Expected to Survive Sex Scandal," *Los Angeles Times,* July 26, 1976, part 1, p. 1.

9. Clapp, *The Congressman: His Job As He Sees It,* p. 94.

Chapter 6. Back to the Vanishing Marginals

1. Richard Fenno, *Home Style* (Boston: Little, Brown, 1978), chap. 6.

Chapter 7. Some Circumstantial Evidence

1. At the time of this writing (94th Congress) only seven congressmen reported that their district offices were not open while they were in Washington. The seven were Evins (Democrat) of Tennessee, elected in 1946, Jones (Democrat) of Alabama, elected in 1946, Mahon (Democrat) of Texas, elected in 1934, Sikes (Democrat) of Florida, elected in 1944, Stevens (Democrat) of Georgia, elected in 1960, Teague (Democrat) of Texas, elected in 1946, and Waggoner (Democrat) of Louisiana, elected in 1961. Note that these holdouts were exclusively southern Democrats and generally senior (five of the seven were elected before 1950). It is perhaps worth pointing out that three (Jones, Teague, and Mahon) were committee chairman, and a fourth (Waggoner) has served in the elective leadership (caucus chairman). Given these internal responsibilities they might be expected to operate large district staff operations to take up the slack. Apparently, though, they didn't do it in the 1940s so don't intend to start now. In Fenno's terms they continue to follow home styles established in a simpler era.

2. Kenneth Olson, "The Service Function of the United States Congress," in *Congress: The First Branch of Government* (Washington: American Enterprise Institute, 1966), p. 344.

3. For additional data and discussion see Cover, "One Good Term Deserves Another."

4. *How to Succeed in Politics* (New York: McFadden Books, 1964), p. 20.

5. Norman Ornstein, "Causes and Consequences of Congressional Change: Subcommittee Reforms in the House of Representatives," in Ornstein, *Congress in Change,* pp. 88–114.

6. Douglas Cater, *Power in Washington* (New York: Random House, 1964); Ernest Griffith, *Congress: Its Contemporary Role* (New York: University Press, 1961); Eugene Eidenberg and Roy Morey, *An Act of Congress* (New York: Norton, 1969).

7. Randall Ripley, *Congress: Process and Policy* (New York: Norton, 1975), pp. 251–52.

8. Kenneth Shepsle, *The Giant Jigsaw Puzzle.*

9. For background discussion see G. R. Pipe, "Congressional Liaison: The Executive Branch Consolidates Its Relations with Congress," *Public Administration Review* 26 (1966): 14–24.

10. Edward de Grazia, "Congressional Liaison—An Inquiry into Its Meaning for Congress," in *Congress: The First Branch,* p. 315.

11. Ibid., p. 314.

12. Randall Ripley, *Party Leaders in the House of Representatives* (Washington, D.C.: Brookings Institution, 1967).

Chapter 8. Alternative Views

1. Representative Barber Conable, *Washington Report,* March 9, 1976.

2. Harold Seidman, *Politics, Position and Power: The Dynamics of Federal Organization,* 2d ed. (New York: Oxford University Press, 1975).

3. Clapp, *The Congressman: His Job As He Sees It,* p. 86.

4. Charles Peters discusses this and other examples in "Firemen First," *Washington Monthly,* March 1976: 8–11. For additional background see "Amtrak Plight," *Congressional Quarterly Weekly Report,* May 29, 1976: 1,365–70.

5. For an accounting of the maneuverings surrounding the O'Neill amendments see *Congressional Quarterly Weekly Report,* April 17, 1976: 932–33, and May 15, 1976: 1,161–63.

6. Vernon Jordan, "'New Minimalism' Threatens the Poor," *Los Angeles Times,* May 6, 1976, part 2, p. 7.

Chapter 9. What Lies Ahead?

1. An aide to Representative John Anderson, the Republican conference chairman, stated the problem concisely: "If effective oversight turns up an inef-

fective program which results in its proposed elimination, the greatest hue and cry goes up from those with a vested interest in the program, and not from taxpayers overjoyed at the prospect of reduced federal spending,'' (quoted in *Congressional Quarterly Weekly Report*, March 22, 1975: 595).

2. Herbert Kaufman, *Are Government Organizations Immortal?* (Washington, D.C.: Brookings Institution, 1976).

3. Quoted in *Lansing State Journal*, February 29, 1976, p. A-4.

4. Quoted in Stuart Auerbach, ''Frustrated Congressman Quitting,'' *Washington Post*, December 27, 1975, p. A-1. Since retiring, Hastings has been convicted of operating a payroll kickback scheme in his Washington office.

Introduction to Part Two

1. For a book-length treatment that divides the development of Congress into three eras—party government, committee government, and subcommittee government—see Lawrence Dodd and Richard Schott, *Congress and the Administrative State* (New York: Wiley, 1979). For a lucid treatment that brings the discussion into the 1980s, see Kenneth Shepsle, ''The Changing Textbook Congress,'' in John Chubb and Paul Peterson, eds., *Can the Government Govern?* (Washington, D.C.: Brookings Institution, 1989).

2. See John Ferejohn and Randall Calvert, ''Presidential Coattails in Historical Perspective,'' *American Journal of Political Science* 28 (Feb. 1984): 127–46; and David Brady and Morris Fiorina, ''Ruptured Legacy: Presidential-Congressional Relations in Historical Perspective,'' in Larry Berman, ed., *The Reagan Imprint* (Baltimore: Johns Hopkins University Press, 1989). On economic conditions in House elections, see Benjamin Radcliff, ''Solving a Puzzle: Aggregate Analysis and Economic Voting Revisited,'' *Journal of Politics* 50 (1988): 440–58.

3. Despite his impressive victory in 1988, George Bush entered the White House with a smaller proportion of his party in the House than any president in history. Of the 245 Democratic incumbents who ran for reelection, only 2 were defeated.

4. This is the central thesis of the research reported in Bruce Cain, John Ferejohn, and Morris Fiorina, *The Personal Vote: Constituency Service and Electoral Independence* (Cambridge, Mass.: Harvard University Press, 1987). David W. Brady applies this argument to the subject of electoral realignment in his *Critical Elections and Congressional Policy Making* (Stanford, Calif.: Stanford University Press, 1988).

5. For accounts and assessments of the transformation of the nominating process, see Austin Ranney, *Curing the Mischiefs of Faction* (Berkeley: Univer-

sity of California Press, 1975), and Nelson Polsby, *Consequences of Party Reform* (New York: Oxford University Press, 1983).

6. I would like to thank Jeffrey Berry, Gary Jacobson, Keith Krehbiel, and Steven S. Smith, who commented on some or all of the following chapters. None of them bears any blame for errors of fact or interpretation that remain.

Chapter 10. Some More-than-Circumstantial Evidence

1. The research community is indebted to Richard S. Beth for two excellent reviews of this extensive literature. See his "Incumbency Advantage and Incumbency Resources: Recent Articles," *Congress and the Presidency* 9 (1981–82): 119–36; and "Recent Research on 'Incumbency Advantage' in House Elections: Part II," *Congress and the Presidency* 11 (1984): 211–24.

2. To update table 5, in the 100th Congress personal staffs of representatives number about 7,500, more than 40 percent are assigned to district offices, and almost all congressmen have multiple district offices that are open year-round. For further details see Norman J. Ornstein, Thomas E. Mann, and Michael J. Malbin, *Vital Statistics on Congress, 1987–88* (Washington, D.C.: Congressional Quarterly, 1989), chap. 5.

3. Cain, Ferejohn, and Fiorina, *The Personal Vote,* chap. 3.

4. Fortunately, the 1958 study as well as the later studies were conducted under the auspices of the same organization, the Institute for Social Research at the University of Michigan. Thus, basic procedures remained constant across the studies, though question wording differed in places. For a detailed discussion of the election studies and the findings surveyed in the text, see my "Congressmen and Their Constituencies: 1958 and 1978," in Dennis Hale, ed., *Proceedings of the Thomas P. O'Neill Jr. Symposium on the U.S. Congress* (Boston: Eusey Press, 1982), pp. 33–64. Neither the Institute for Social Research nor the National Election Studies organization, which has conducted the studies since 1978, bears any responsibility for my interpretations of this data.

5. These and other details of casework are discussed in Cain, Ferejohn, and Fiorina, *The Personal Vote,* chap. 2.

6. Calculations appear in Fiorina, "Some Problems in Studying the Effects of Resource Allocation in Congressional Elections," *American Journal of Political Science* 25 (Aug. 1981): 543–67.

7. The comments were categorized by the staff of the survey organization. For details, see Fiorina, "Congressmen and Their Constituencies."

8. Again, the comments were categorized by the survey organization. There are not many negative comments to analyze, and no particular pattern emerges. For details, see Fiorina, "Congressmen and Their Constituencies."

9. This tentative finding is subject to a further caveat. Gary Jacobson notes that in the 1982 and 1984 NES surveys references to party are about twice as common as in the 1978 and 1980 surveys. Democrats in 1982 and Republicans in 1984 had obvious reasons to inject a party theme into their campaign. See Jacobson, *The Politics of Congressional Elections*, pp. 132–33.

10. This conclusion is based on probit analyses of voting decisions reported in Fiorina, "Congressmen and Their Constituencies." These analyses estimate the independent impact of each factor while holding other relevant factors constant.

11. Cain, Ferejohn, and Fiorina, *The Personal Vote,* chap. 3.

12. Fiorina, "Some Problems," table 1.

13. Cain, Ferejohn, and I formulated an index of casework from four pieces of information: whether the congressional office actively solicits cases from constituents, whether it publicizes successful cases, whether it handles cases involving state and local government, and whether it has a particularly large number of caseworkers (the top third of all offices). Two variables are positively related to variations in casework aggressiveness as measured by this index: previous election margin and seniority. For details, see Cain, Ferejohn, and Fiorina, "The Constituency Component: A Comparison of Service in Great Britain and the United States," *Comparative Political Studies* 16 (1983): 67–91.

14. See the articles by Thomas Mann and Raymond Wolfinger, Alan Abramowitz, and Barbara Hinckley in the *American Political Science Review* 74 (1980).

15. Cain, Ferejohn, and Fiorina, *The Personal Vote.*

16. Norman Ornstein, "The Reelection Phenomenon: Unsolved." *Washington Post,* May 19, 1977.

17. Steven H. Schiff and Steven S. Smith, "Generational Change and the Allocation of Staff in the U.S. Congress," *Legislative Studies Quarterly* 3 (1983): 457–67.

18. John Johannes, *To Serve the People: Congress and Constituency Service* (Lincoln: University of Nebraska Press, 1984); Cain, Ferejohn, and Fiorina, *The Personal Vote,* chap. 2.

19. Roger H. Davidson and Walter J. Oleszek, *Congress and Its Members* (Washington, D. C.: Congressional Quarterly Press, 1985), p. 436.

20. Michael Malbin, *Unelected Representatives* (New York: Basic Books, 1980).

21. Mayhew, *Congress: The Electoral Connection.*

22. Constituents, incidentally, have become significantly more likely to prefer that representatives follow district wishes rather than make decisions based on their own best judgment; see Fiorina, "Congressmen and Their Constituencies," table 5.

23. Thomas Mann, *Unsafe at Any Margin* (Washington, D.C.: American Enterprise, 1977).

24. Gary Jacobson, "Running Scared: Elections and Congressional Politics

in the 1980s,'' in Mathew McCubbins and Terry Sullivan, eds., *Congress: Structure and Policy* (Cambridge: Cambridge University Press, 1987), pp. 39–81; and ''The Marginals Never Vanished,'' *American Journal of Political Science* 31 (1987): 126–41.

25. That is, actual service and resource levels are positively related to evaluations of member job performance and to expectations that members would be helpful if the occasion arose, and such evaluations of members are strongly related to reported vote. See Cain, Ferejohn, and Fiorina, *The Personal Vote*, chap. 6.

26. For more details and full citations see Cain, Ferejohn, and Fiorina, *The Personal Vote*, chap. 5.

27. Ibid., chap. 5.

28. Gary Jacobson, *Money in Congressional Elections* (New Haven: Yale University Press, 1980), p. xvii.

29. For the technically inclined, the construction of suitable instrumental variables is the difficulty. Estimation requires the use of variables that relate to electoral outcomes but not to the factors believed to influence those outcomes (campaign spending, casework, etc.) and vice versa. Obviously, few such variables can be found. Moreover, specification of the models is still in an ad hoc stage. In particular, we do not know enough about the processes that generate strong or weak challengers.

Chapter 11. Confusions and Clarifications

1. Gary Jacobson has since pointed out that reelection rates went up even less—only about 1 percent during the 1960s. Of course, they were extremely high—above 90 percent—to begin with. Over a slightly longer period, reelection rates have risen from about 91 percent in the 1946–64 period to a bit less than 95 percent in the 1966–86 period. For discussion, see Jacobson, ''The Marginals Never Vanished''; Steven Ansolabehere, David Brady and Morris Fiorina, ''The Marginals Never Vanished?'' (forthcoming).

2. Cain, Ferejohn, and Fiorina, *The Personal Vote*, chap. 7.

3. In Great Britain, MPs attach great significance to their service activities, though the influence of such activities on the vote is minimal compared to what it is in the United States. But in the highly centralized, party-structured British system, constituency service is one of the few things that the individual MP controls. See Cain, Ferejohn, and Fiorina, *The Personal Vote*, chap. 3.

4. For a general discussion, see Thomas Mann, ''Is the House of Representatives Unresponsive to Political Change?'', in A. James Reichley, ed., *Elections American Style* (Washington, D.C.: Brookings Institution, 1987), pp. 269–75. Some recent academic studies include Amihai Glazer, Bernard Grofman, and Marc Robbins, ''Partisan and Incumbency Effects of 1970s Congressional Re-

districting," *American Journal of Political Science* 31 (Aug. 1987): 680–707; and Richard Born, "Partisan Intentions and Election Day Realities in the Congressional Redistricting Process," *American Political Science Review* 79 (June 1985): 305–19.

5. On the comparative visibility of incumbents across time, see Fiorina, "Congressmen and Their Constituencies." In the survey conducted in 1978, incumbent congressmen were actually somewhat *less* well known than in the 1958 survey.

6. See table 3, which shows that popular perceptions of members of Congress have changed over time.

7. Recall the discussion in the preceding chapter.

8. See Jacobson, "Running Scared."

9. The seminal work on campaign finance is Jacobson, *Money in Congressional Elections*. For a more recent discussion see his "Money and Votes Reconsidered: Congressional Elections, 1972–1982," *Public Choice* 47 (1985): 7–62.

10. Barbara Hinckley, "The American Voter in Congressional Elections," *American Political Science Review* 74 (1980): 641–50; Lyn Ragsdale, "Incumbent Popularity, Challenger Invisibility, and Congressional Voters," *Legislative Studies Quarterly* 6 (1981): 201–18.

11. Gary Jacobson reports that, at least as measured by previous electoral experience, challenger quality did not decline over this period (letter to author, Dec. 30, 1988).

12. Jon Bond, Gary Covington, and Richard Fleisher, "Explaining Challenger Quality in Congressional Elections," *Journal of Politics* 47 (1985): 510–29. For an argument that challenger quality is not well measured in most studies, see Donald Green and Jonathan Krasno, "Salvation for the Spendthrift Incumbent: Reestimating the Effects of Campaign Spending in House Elections," *American Journal of Political Science* 32 (1988): 884–907.

13. Because this perspective dominates the field of economics, the rational-choice approach is sometimes called the "economic" approach to politics. It should be noted that the rational-choice approach does not presume that human beings are all-knowing supercomputers. What is rational is defined relative to the context. For example, in complex, highly uncertain situations where information is unavailable or otherwise costly, rational behavior may entail acting in accord with simple rules of thumb.

14. Anthony Down, *An Economic Theory of Democracy* (New York: Harper and Row, 1957), p. 37.

15. Richard Fenno analyzes congressional committee behavior in terms of three goals: reelection, power in the House, and policy preferences. But Fenno does not use the full generality of this formulation. He assumes that committees allow differential opportunities to satisfy different goals; thus, self-selection leads one goal to predominate among the members of one committee, a different

goal among the members of a second committee, and so forth. See his *Congressmen in Committees* (Boston: Little, Brown, 1973).

16. Thus, rational-choice analysts have paid little attention to the behavior of judges—there is no obvious motive that plausibly can be attributed to judges.

17. To be scrupulously fair to the critics, there are a number of subschools operating under the "rational-choice" rubric, some of which provide some grounds for the straw man attacked by the critics. For example, Chicago-school political economy sometimes does equate self-interest with wealth maximization. And with less regularity, Virginia-school public-choice analyses sometimes adopt an overly grim perspective on government behavior. Critics seldom seek to understand the variations evident in rational-choice analyses, simply lumping them together and ascribing to all of them the characteristics they like least in any of them.

18. The potential for trade-off between electoral and other goals was explicitly recognized in the distinction between "maximizers and maintainers" that I drew in *Representatives, Roll Calls and Constituencies*, chap. 2.

19. Kennedy's once-popular *Profiles in Courage* (New York: Harper and Row, 1955) describes courageous political actions by U.S. senators.

20. Martha Derthick and Paul J. Quirk, *The Politics of Regulation* (Washington, D.C.: Brookings Institution, 1985).

21. One might note, too, that the permanent staff of the agency was not nearly so enthused about its abolition as were the political appointees.

22. On occasion voters are assumed to be motivated by broader "ideological" beliefs, as with environmentalists, animal rights activists, and so forth. This illustrates my earlier observation that rational-choice analyses can proceed with any specification of goals.

23. At this point the obvious question arises: what about professors? If people are self-interested, why assume that professors are serving any interest other than their own? That is, in fact, the proper assumption to make. But, happily, the organization of higher education channels professorial self-interest in socially desirable directions. That is, we are well regarded (and well rewarded) to the degree that we are open-minded, candid, and perceptive observers and critics.

24. Thus, Paul Quirk discounts the popular argument that regulators' decisions are biased by their expectations of future employment in the industries they regulate. His findings are based on personal interviews. Call me cynical, but if I were out to make a bundle trading on my connections in government, I would be highly circumspect in what I said to interviewers. Quirk may be correct, but it will take more than interview evidence to convince me. Where incentives are concerned, what people do is more informative than what they say. See Quirk's *Industry Influence in Federal Regulatory Agencies* (Princeton, N.J.: Princeton University Press, 1981), pp. 164–74.

25. Recently, the Congress agreed to set up a commission that would recommend the closure of outdated military bases. No more than twenty-five of the nation's installations are expected to be closed. This uncharacteristic congressional action was enough to make Steven Kelman see "public spirit" breaking out all over. But the point is that this fairly minor action was highly uncharacteristic. That is why the newspapers found it worthy of front-page coverage. As *Congressional Quarterly* noted, "The conference report on S 2749 easily passed both houses on October 12, with members of both parties citing it as a rare instance of congressional willingness to subordinate constituency interests in preserving local payrolls to a broader national interest in trimming the deficit." Should our accounts of congressional politics be premised on the exceptions or the norm? See Kelman, "Public Spirit Lives, Even in Congress," *Wall Street Journal*, Sept. 13, 1988; and Pat Towell, "Hill Paves Way for Closing Old Bases," *Congressional Quarterly Weekly Report* 46 (Oct. 15, 1988): 2,999.

26. Steven Kelman, "Public Choice and Public Spirit," *The Public Interest* 87 (1987): 81–94.

27. Benjamin Wright, "*The Federalist* and the Nature of Political Man," *Ethics* 59 (1949): 1–31.

28. "*The Federalist* seeks to ground republican government on the most reliable aspect of human nature: self-interest. By self-interest, Publius means that most men, if left alone, will naturally seek to satisfy their own interests and desires, rather than look to the well being of the whole" (Jean Yarbrough, "The Federalist," *This Constitution* 16 [Fall 1987]: 5).

29. Madison exempts the Constitutional Convention from this judgment, placing it among the few lustrous exceptions to his generalization. Possibly he was correct; certainly it was in his interest to make the claim.

30. The Founders' view of human nature was not relentlessly negative. At one point Madison (no. 55) observes that "as there is a degree of depravity in mankind which requires a certain degree of circumspection and distrust, so there are other qualities in human nature which justify a certain portion of esteem and confidence. Republican government presupposes the existence of these qualities in a higher degree than any other form." The Founders did not deny that human beings possessed higher qualities, but they warned that these were neither so powerful nor so widespread as to serve as the basis for government. As Madison observes elsewhere (no. 42), "The mild voice of reason, pleading the cause of an enlarged and permanent interest, is but too often drowned, before public bodies as well as individuals, by the clamors of an impatient avidity for immediate and immoderate gains." In short, self-interest may not always overcome virtue, but that's the way to bet.

31. Tocqueville, *Democracy in America* (New York: Vintage, 1945), p. 142.

32. Bryce goes on to comment that "it is much to be wished that in every

country public spirit were the chief motive propelling men into public life. But is it so anywhere now? Has it been so at any time in a nation's history? Let anyone in England . . . ask himself how many of those whom he knows as mixing in the public life of his own country have entered it from motives primarily patriotic, how many have been actuated by the love of fame or power, the hope of advancing their social pretensions or their business relations.'' Bryce does not condemn human nature; rather, as a good political scientist he seeks to explain the recruitment of particular types of people into public life and deduce the consequences of politics as it is for the operation of the American system. See James Bryce, *The American Commonwealth* (London: Macmillan, 1988), pp. 391 and 404.

33. See, for example, Arthur Bentley, *The Process of Government* (Evanston, Ill.: Principia Press, 1949).

34. A noteworthy exception is Joseph Schlesinger, who makes the positive case for electoral self-interest: ''The desire for election and, more important, for reelection becomes the electorate's restraint upon its public officials. No more irresponsible government is imaginable than one of high-minded men unconcerned for their political futures.'' (*Ambition in Politics* [Chicago: Rand McNally, 1966], p. 2).

35. On particularized interests and credit claiming, see Mayhew, *Congress: The Electoral Connection*, pp. 52–61.

36. See R. Douglas Arnold, *Congress and the Bureaucracy: A Theory of Influence* (New Haven: Yale University Press, 1979); and Morris Fiorina and Roger Noll, ''Majority Rule Models and Legislative Elections,'' *Journal of Politics* 41 (1979): 1,081–1,104.

37. See Arnold, *Congress and the Bureaucracy*.

38. See Samuel Beer, ''The Adoption of General Revenue Sharing,'' *Public Policy* 24 (1976): 190–94.

39. Revenue sharing was one of the few major federal programs abolished (rather than scaled down) during the Reagan years. Congressmen took advantage of budget problems to do what they would have like to do earlier.

40. David Price, *Who Makes the Laws?* (Cambridge, Mass.: Schenkman, 1972), pp. 28–29.

41. R. Douglas Arnold proposes that congressional policy-making be analyzed according to a tripartite scheme of general benefits, group benefits, and local benefits. See his ''Logic of Congressional Action'' (unpublished manuscript).

42. R. Kent Weaver, *Automatic Government: The Politics of Indexation* (Washington, D.C.: Brookings Institution, 1988).

43. The example game can be played by anyone with the patience to work through the sources. For example, at about the same time that Congress was preparing to close some military bases, Representative Charles Stenholm (D.,

Texas) offered a "truth in legislation" proposal that would have required committee reports to flag legislative provisions with ten or fewer beneficiaries, and in addition to *identify* the provisions' authors and beneficiaries. Stenholm's proposal lost 137-32, Apparently the public spirit took a walk on this one. See Janet Hook, "House Outlook for 1989: More Partisan Strife," *Congressional Quarterly Weekly Report*, Dec. 10, 1988: 3,471.

44. Kelman, "Public Choice and Public Spirit," 85.

Chapter 12. Underemphases and New Developments

1. For an argument that this rise was more apparent than real, see Bruce Keith et al., "The Myth of the Independent Voter" (unpublished manuscript).

2. Personal communication, 1977.

3. John Alford and David Brady provide a comprehensive historical treatment of congressional election returns in "Partisan and Incumbent Advantage in U.S. House Elections, 1846–1986" (forthcoming).

4. In 1848 a three-way presidential race resulted in the election of Whig Zachary Taylor with Democratic majorities in both houses. In 1876 Republican Rutherford B. Hayes was eventually declared the presidential winner, while the Democrats captured the House. But since Samuel Tilden apparently won the popular vote for the presidency, this was not clearly a split result.

5. This is not a hypothetical argument. In 1962, for example, the Daley organization in Chicago summoned Rep. Sydney Yates home to take on Senate Minority Leader Everett Dirksen. Yates's prospects were not good, but the organization was not about to concede Dirksen an easy victory that might have repurcussions further down the ticket. Yates ran a good race but lost, as expected. He was given a position as U.S. representative to a UN organization. Then, in 1964, the man holding Yates's old seat was given a state judgeship and Yates returned to Congress. He sacrificed his seniority, but not his career or financial condition.

6. Larry Dodd develops a cynical theory that incorporates such a dynamic; see his "Theory of Congressional Cycles," p. 183n5.

7. That is, incumbents have always done better than nonincumbents, but mainly because on average they come from districts where their party has an advantage: The advantage is partisan rather than personal. After analyzing all House election returns from 1846 to 1986, Alford and Brady find that a distinct personal advantage emerges only in the 1960s; see their "Partisan and Incumbent Advantage."

8. For an excellent treatment of the national parties in relation to congressional elections, see Paul Herrnson, *Party Campaigning in the 1980s* (Cambridge, Mass.: Harvard University Press, 1988).

9. Stephen Frantzich, *Political Parties: The Technological Age* (White Plains, N.Y.: Longman, 1989).

10. Of course, a rational party would not pressure its members to the point where they would seriously risk losing their seats to the other party.

11. See Larry Sabato, *The Party's Just Begun* (Glenview, Ill.: Scott, Foresman, 1988), esp. chap. 7.

12. The quotation marks are in recognition of the fact that reform is in the eye of the beholder. One person's reform can be another's travesty of justice.

13. Most, not all. The caveat reflects two considerations. First, Mark Westlye has presented evidence that small-state senate elections do not differ from House elections as much as large-state senate elections. Second, there are occasional expensive and hard-fought House elections that at least on the surface resemble typical Senate contests. See his "Competitiveness of Senate Seats and Voting Behavior in Senate Elections," *American Journal of Political Science* 27 (1983): 253–83.

14. To reiterate, these assertions are inferences drawn from media coverage of Senate campaigns, case studies, and a few empirical studies. As noted, we still do not have the kind of data for Senate elections that would enable us to put these assertions on a solid footing. The National Elections Studies organization carried out the first wave of a national study of Senate elections in the fall of 1988, with additional waves tentatively planned for 1990 and 1992. These studies for the first time will provide data comparable to that available for the House since 1978.

15. Stephen Hess finds that the lion's share of national press coverage goes to more senior senators who occupy positions of institutional responsibility, such as the chairmanships of important committees and subcommittees. See *The Ultimate Insiders* (Washington, D.C.: Brookings Institution, 1986).

16. Charges that he was more concerned with Angola than with California appeared to play a part in former Senator John Tunney's 1976 loss to Republican S. I. Hayakawa. The case was similar for former Senator Dick Clark of Iowa, formerly chair of the Foreign Relations Subcommittee on Africa.

17. Interestingly, though, when term length and average reelection rates are compounded, senators have expected career lengths just as long as representatives. See Amihai Glazer and Bernard Grofman, "Two Plus Two Equals Six: Tenure in Office of Senators and Representatives, 1953–1983," *Legislative Studies Quarterly* 12 (1987): 555–64.

18. Fiorina, "The Presidency and Congress," in Michael Nelson, ed., *The Presidency and the Political System* (Washington, D.C.: Congressional Quarterly Press, 1988), pp. 426–28.

19. Gary Jacobson's analysis of the 1988 outcomes is fully consistent with this characterization. See "Congress: A Singular Continuity," in Michael

Nelson, ed., *The Elections of 1988* (Washington, D.C.: Congressional Quarterly Press, 1989).

20. Fiorina, "The Case of the Vanishing Marginals: The Bureaucracy Did It," *American Political Science Review* 71 (1977): 180n5.

21. Fox and Hammond, *Congressional Staffs: The Invisible Force in American Law Making* (New York: Free Press, 1977); Salisbury and Shepsle, "Congressional Staff Turnover and the Ties that Bind," *American Political Science Review* 75 (1981): 381–96; Loomis, "The Congressional Office as a Small (?) Business: New Members Set up Shop," *Publius* 9 (1979): 35–55; Patterson, "The Professional Staffs of Congressional Committees," *Administrative Science Quarterly* 15 (1970): 22–37; and Malbin, *Unelected Representatives* (New York: Basic Books, 1980).

22. The most complete figures on staff (as well as most other subjects) can be found in Ornstein, Mann, and Malbin, *Vital Statistics on Congress, 1987–1988*.

23. "From the numbers, it seems obvious that most of the members' new personal staff aides do constituency-related work that may help an incumbent win reelection but has little to do with the legislative process" (Michael Malbin, "Delegation, Deliberation, and the New Role of Congressional Staff," in Thomas Mann and Norman Ornstein, eds., *The New Congress* [Washington, D.C.: American Enterprise Institute, 1981], p. 143).

24. Malbin, *Unelected Representatives,* pp. 6–7.

25. In our comparative research on the British House of Commons, one of the most understaffed legislatures in the world, a number of MPs denied any wish for more staff, claiming that staff would create more new work than they could accomplish. We regarded such views as curmudgeonly at the time, but in view of recent congressional history, they may have been prescient.

26. *The Federalist,* no. 63.

27. The first edition of *Keystone* argues that bureaucrats are not so unaccountable as popularly believed. Still, they are not as subject to the whims of individual congressmen as staff directly employed by congressmen. As for judges, they are indeed largely unaccountable actors. Some believe this is as it should be; others have their doubts.

28. For a discussion of national policy-making oriented around the subgovernment concept, see Randall Ripley and Grace Franklin, *Congress, the Bureaucracy, and Public Policy,* 4th ed. (Chicago: Dorsey Press, 1987).

29. This is the also the judgment of a prominent scholar of interest groups, Jeffrey Berry. See his "Subgovernments, Issue Networks, and Political Conflict," in Richard Harris and Sidney Milkis, eds., *Remaking American Politics* (Boulder, Colo.: Westview, 1989), pp. 239–60.

30. Thomas Gais, Mark Peterson, and Jack Walker, "Interest Groups, Iron

Triangles and Representative Institutions in American National Government,'' *British Journal of Political Science* 14 (1984): 161–85.

31. Dodd and Schott, *Congress and the Administrative State* (New York: Wiley, 1979), pp. 174–79.

32. The best description of these developments can be found in Steven S. Smith, *Call to Order: Floor Politics in the House and Senate* (Washington, D.C.: Brookings Institution, 1989).

33. For a good recent view of these and other congressional developments, see Shepsle, ''The Changing Textbook Congress.''

34. Consistent with this view, Jeffrey Berry argues that the erosion of subgovernment politics was clearly underway during the Carter years (''Subgovernments, Issue Networks, and Political Conflict'').

35. Gary Jacobson, ''The Effects of Campaign Spending in Congressional Elections,'' *American Political Science Review* 72 (1978): 469–91; and *Money in Congressional Elections*.

36. See, for example, Elizabeth Drew, *Politics and Money: The New Road to Corruption* (New York: Macmillan, 1983).

37. Excellent surveys of the issues can be found in the articles included in Michael Malbin, ed., *Money and Politics in the United States* (Washington, D.C.: American Enterprise Institute, 1984); and in Frank J. Sorauf, *Money in American Elections* (Glenview, Ill.: Scott, Foresman, 1988).

38. Note that party contributions appear to be an increasingly small proportion of the total. As noted earlier in the chapter, however, parties make large ''coordinated'' expenditures that do not appear in these tabulations. Moreover, to some degree parties coordinate PAC contributing.

39. ''Comparing Contributions to U.S. House Candidates from Outside Their Districts,'' *Legislative Studies Quarterly* 13 (1988): 83–104.

40. Grenzke's careful procedures are subject to a further caveat. Many PACs have Washington addresses and are thus by definition out of state. But if they make contributions to candidates in proportion to the PAC contributions coming from their areas, then some money counted as nonlocal is actually local.

41. This is a broad-brush generalization, to be sure. For a detailed treatment that provides fine differentiations, see Theodore Eismeier and Philip Pollock, ''Political Action Committees: Varieties of Organization and Strategy,'' in Malbin, *Money and Politics*.

42. Kay Schlozman and John Tierney raise the same question in their *Organized Interests and American Democracy* (New York: Harper and Row, 1986), p. 258.

43. Frank Wright, ''The Dairy Lobby Buys the Cream of the Congress,'' *Washington Monthly* 3 (1971): 17–21.

44. The same may be true for committees like Banking that deal in esoteric subjects, such as financial deregulation.

45. "PAC Gifts to Tax-Writers Double," *Congressional Quarterly Weekly Report,* Feb. 15, 1986: 297.

Chapter 13. Looking Back and Looking Ahead

1. Stephen Frantzich, "Opting Out: Retirement from the House of Representatives," *American Politics Quarterly* 6 (1978): 251–73; Joseph Cooper and William West, "The Congressional Career in the 1970s," in Lawrence C. Dodd and Bruce I. Oppenheimer, eds., *Congress Reconsidered,* 2d. ed. (Washington, D.C.: Congressional Quarterly Press, 1981).

2. While the level of party cohesion within the Congress increased in the 1980s, I doubt that it signifies any new era of unified congressional parties. The decline in southern Democratic districts and the increased level of black voting in others has made southern Democrats less distinct from northerners. More generally, the Reagan administration and its confrontational style must be factored in.

3. On the disparity between objective and subjective security, see Fenno, *Home Style,* pp. 8–18.

4. Jacobson, "Running Scared" and "The Marginals Never Vanished."

5. Mayhew, *Congress: The Electoral Connection,* pp. 36–37.

6. This is not to deny that there have been some marginal improvements in congressional operating procedures. In particular, from the standpoint of this book's argument, anything that strengthens the hand of the party leadership raises the probability that public policies can avoid the "death of a thousand cuts" that is too often their fate.

7. At the national level the citizenry can end-run Congress by electing a hostile president or adopting a constitutional amendment (ratified by three-fourths of the states). At the state level many citizens enjoy an additional alternative: the initiative. In California, for example, Proposition 13 (1978) was an end-run of the legislature (and the governor). Popular frustration with the property tax had become palpable, but the legislature refused to act, largely because of the opposition of the Democratic party's organized constituency groups. Eventually, a frustrated electorate opted for a highly imperfect form of relief.

8. I continue to believe that Carter has shouldered too much of the blame for the Democratic party's dismal performance of 1976–80. And certainly it is hard to understand the degree of emotional antagonism some academics feel toward Carter. For a balanced view of the Carter presidency and its difficulties with Congress, see Charles O. Jones, *The Trusteeship Presidency* (Baton Rouge: Louisiana State University Press, 1988).

9. The term was originally applied to nineteenth-century rivers and harbors bills (William Safire, *Safire's Political Dictionary* [New York: Random House, 1978], p. 553).

10. For a summary of the politics of the water projects fights, see *Congressional Quarterly Almanac* (Washington, D.C.: Congressional Quarterly, 1977), pp. 650–59.

11. The standard exceptions were welfare and the space program.

12. The more technically inclined reader may note that the situation is reminiscent of an n-person prisoner's dilemma in game theory, or more generally, of an exploitation of the commons problem. For a general discussion, see Russell Hardin, *Collective Action* (Baltimore: Johns Hopkins University Press, 1982).

13. David Stockman, *The Triumph of Politics* (New York: Harper and Row, 1986), pp. 376–77.

14. John Chubb, "Federalism and the Bias for Centralization," in John E. Chubb and Paul E. Peterson, eds., *New Directions in American Politics* (Washington, D.C.: Brookings Institution, 1985), pp. 286–92.

15. *Congressional Quarterly* provides an obituary for a recent casualty: "After eight years of using all its might to kill congressionally treasured Urban Development Action Grants (UDAGs), the lame-duck Reagan administration would finally get its way in House and Senate spending bills now in the works. "There is no other way," said Rep. Edward P. Boland, D-Mass. " . . . After years of defending it, Boland called UDAG "the lowest priority" in the House bill." The example is telling on at least three accounts. First, it illustrates Chubb's point that Congress managed to keep program structures intact even while program funds dwindled. Second, it demonstrates that the Reagan administration did manage to take Congress head-on and win in some instances. But third, it illustrates the difficulty and time involved in overcoming congressional incentives. See Phil Kuntz, *Congressional Quarterly Weekly Report*, June 18, 1988: 1,688–89.

16. Daniel P. Moynihan, *Came the Revolution* (New York: Harcourt, Brace and Jovanovich, 1988). At this point it is not especially important whether the deficits were consciously planned from the beginning. Even if not planned, after the fact of the deficits became evident, it is certainly reasonable to suspect that the Reaganauts looked at the bright side (squeezing the domestic sector) and decided that, on balance, continued large deficits were preferable to raising taxes or cutting defense spending.

17. See Mann, "Is the House of Representatives Unresponsive to Political Change?"

18. Around the world, in single-member district, simple plurality electoral

systems, swing ratios tend to fall in the range 2-4: vote gains are magnified when translated into seat gains.

19. The calculations and much of this discussion are based on Ansolabehere, Brady, and Fiorina, "The Marginals Never Vanished?"

20. John W. Mashek, "Atwater Urges Republicans to Reach Out to Minorities," *Boston Globe,* Jan. 19, 1989: 14. Both Lee Atwater and Fahrenkopf point to gerrymandering as the root of their congressional difficulties. As noted in chapter 11, however, gerrymandering is not the problem. Gerrymandering is becoming for Republicans what "dull presidential nominees" have become for Democrats—a convenient, incorrect, and self-justifying explanation for repeated political failure.

21. House Democrats united behind an alternative set of budget cuts proposed by the Democratic members of the Budget Committee, and an alternative tax cut proposed by the Democratic members of Ways and Means.

22. Thus, David Broder ("Housecleaning Is Needed") mentions approvingly the proposal of a Republican congressman, Thomas Petri of Wisconsin, that has been unable to receive a hearing by the majority.

23. *The Federalist,* no. 51. Today's students, whose political consciousness typically dates back only a decade or so, often have difficulty appreciating the Founders' perspective. A useful assignment is to have them learn the Third Amendment: "No soldier shall, in time of peace, be quartered in any house, without the consent of the owner, nor in time of war, but in a manner to be prescribed by law."

24. As political scientists never tire of pointing out, the Constitution did not establish a separation of powers. It established an arrangement by which separate institutions share power. The formal separation of powers is a myth perpetrated by the legal profession. As James Q. Wilson has observed, Supreme Courts capable of breathtakingly broad interpretations of other constitutional provisions adopt the perspective of seventh-grade civics texts when separation of powers issues arise. One suspects that there is more than a little institutional self-interest in the Court's inconsistency. See Wilson, "Does the Separation of Powers Still Work?" *The Public Interest* 86 (1987): 36–52.

25. *The Federalist,* no. 51.

26. Brady, *Critical Elections and Congressional Policy-Making.*

27. The Nixon tragedy brings up another point. In recent years commentators have remarked on the "criminalization" of political disagreement. Investigations and indictments seem a more common feature of national politics than they were a generation ago. Divided government probably contributes to this tendency. Frustrated executives may explore and exceed the bounds of the permissible in efforts to escape congressional constraints. And without common party ties, hardball politics may escalate to the legal arena. At the very least, divided govern-

ment encourages a full airing of any and all misdeeds, real and imagined. When Nixon apologists attacked the Kennedys and Roosevelt and charged partisan bias, they were at most partly correct. It was not only partisan bias but also unified control that helped save earlier presidents from the consequences of their transgressions.

Index